ON THE
INTERPRETATION OF THE VEDA

ON THE INTERPRETATION OF THE VEDA.

By J. MUIR, Esq.

GYAN

Published by

Gyan Publishing House
5, Ansari Road
Daryaganj, New Delhi-110002
Phone: 011-47034999, 9811692060
E-mail: books@gyanbooks.com

Distribution Network
gyanbooks.com
India, USA, Canada, UK, Australia

ISBN: 978-93-6280-288-0 (HB)
First Published, 1899

2nd Impression 2024

Printed at: Gyan Press, Delhi.

ON THE INTERPRETATION OF THE VEDA
Author: J. MUIR

ON THE

INTERPRETATION OF THE VEDA.

By J. MUIR, Esq.

1899

ON THE

INTERPRETATION OF THE VEDA.

BY J. MUIR, ESQ.

I AM led to make some remarks on the subject of this paper by a passage in Mr. Cowell's preface to the fourth volume of the late Professor Wilson's translation of the Rig-veda, which appears to me unduly to depreciate the services which have already been rendered by those eminent scholars both in Germany and in England who have begun to apply the scientific processes of modern philology to the explanation of this ancient hymn-collection. Mr. Cowell admits (p. vi.),—

"As Vaidik studies progress, and more texts are published and studied, fresh light will be thrown on these records of the ancient world; and we may gradually attain a deeper insight into their meaning than the mediæval Hindus could possess, just as a modern scholar may understand Homer more thoroughly than the Byzantine scholiasts."

But he goes on to say:—

"It is easy to depreciate native commentators, but it is not so easy to supersede them; and while I would by no means uphold Sâyaṇa as infallible, I confess that, in the present early stage of Vaidik studies in Europe, it seems to me the safer course to follow native tradition rather than to accept too readily the arbitrary conjectures which continental scholars so often hazard."

Without considering it necessary to examine, or defend, all the explanations of particular words proposed by the foreign lexicographers alluded to by Mr. Cowell, I yet venture to think that those scholars have been perfectly justified in commencing at once the arduous task of expounding the Veda on the principles of interpretation which they have adopted and enunciated. This task is, no doubt—(as those who undertake it themselves confess)—one which will only be properly accomplished by the critical labours of many scholars, I may even say, of several successive generations. This is clear, if any proof were wanted, from the parallel case of the Old

Testament; on the interpretation of which Hebraists, after all the studies of many centuries, are yet far from having said their last word. But what are those texts, and additional materials and appliances which Mr. Cowell desires to have within reach before we are to suffer ourselves to distrust the authority of native commentators, and to make any efforts to attain that deeper insight into the meaning of the Vedas which he feels to be desirable? The Rig-veda, as every one admits, stands alone in its antiquity, and in the character of its contents, and must therefore, as regards its more peculiar and difficult portions, be interpreted mainly through itself. To apply in another sense the words of its commentator, it shines by its own light, and is self-demonstrating.[1] But the whole text of the Rig-veda Sanhitâ has been already published with the commentary on the first eight books. The texts of the Sâma-veda (which contains only a few verses which are not in the Rig-veda) and of the White Yajur-veda, have also been printed. It is true that only a part of the Black Yajur-veda has yet been given to the world, but there is no reason to suppose that it contains any very large amount of matter which will throw light on the real sense of the older hymns. Besides, we already possess in print the texts of the two most important Brâhmanas, and a portion of a third, so that any aid which can be derived from them is also at our command. But even if additional materials of greater value than are ever likely to be brought to light were still inaccessible, why should not competent scholars proceed at once, with the very considerable means which they already possess, to lay the foundation of a true interpretation of the Rig-veda, leaving the mistakes which they may now commit to be corrected by their own future researches, or by those of their successors, when further helps shall have become available? *Ars longa vita brevis.*

I propose in the course of this paper to show, by a selection of instances from the Nirukta, and from Sâyaṇa's commentary, the unsatisfactory character of the assistance which those works afford for explaining many of the most difficult

[1] See Müller's Rig-veda, vol. i., p. 4, lines 21ff.

passages of the hymns, and the consequent necessity which exists that all the other available resources of philology should be called into requisition to supply their deficiencies. But before proceeding to this part of my task, I wish to allow the representatives of the different schools of Vedic interpretation to state their own opinions on the subject under consideration.

Professor Wilson professes to have based his translation of the hymns of the Rig-veda on the commentary of Sâyaṇa Acharya, who lived in the fourteenth century of the Christian era, and on whose work he remarks that—

> "Although the interpretation of Sâyaṇa may be occasionally questioned, he undoubtedly had a knowledge of his text far beyond the pretensions of any European scholar, and must have been in possession, either through his own learning or that of his assistants, of all the interpretations which had been perpetuated by traditional teaching from the earliest times."—Introduction to Translation of Rig-veda Sanhitâ (published in 1850), vol. i., p. xlix.

And in a note to his translation of the 10th hymn of the 1st Book (vol. i., p. 25) he observes, on certain proposed renderings of Prof. Roth and M. Langlois, that "Sâyaṇa, no doubt, knew much better than either of the European interpreters what the expression intended." In the introduction to his second vol., p. xix. (published in 1854), Prof. Wilson returns to the subject, and remarks, among other things, as follows:—

> "With respect to unusual words, there are no doubt a great number employed in the Veda, and it is possible that the lexicographic significations given by the commentators may be sometimes questionable, sometimes contradictory; but from what other authority can a satisfactory interpretation be derived? It has been supposed that a careful collation of all the passages in which such words occur might lead to a consistent and indisputable interpretation; but this assumes that they have always been employed with precision and uniformity by the original authors, a conclusion that would scarcely be tenable even if the author were one individual, and utterly untenable when, as is the case with the Sûktas, the authors are indefinitely numerous: it is very improbable, therefore, that even such collation would remove all perplexity on this account,

although it might occasionally do so; at any rate such a concordance has still to be established, and until it is effected we may be satisfied with the interpretation given us by the most distinguished native scholars, availing themselves of all the Vaidik learning that had preceded them," etc. etc.

Again in p. xxii. he says :—

"The more unmanageable difficulties are those which are utterly insuperable except by guess: they are not the perplexities of commission, but of omission: not the words or phrases that are given, but those that are left out: the constant recurrence of the abuse of ellipsis and metonymy, requiring not only words, but sometimes sentences, to be supplied by comment or conjecture, before any definite meaning can be given to the expressions that occur. . . . . . It may not always require extraordinary ingenuity to hit upon what is intended by such elliptical expressions from correlative terms or context; but such a mode of interpretation by European scholars, whose ordinary train of thinking runs in a very different channel from that of Indian scholarship, can scarcely claim equal authority with the latter," etc.

In regard to one of these elliptical texts, Prof. Wilson expresses himself very unhesitatingly when he says (p. xxiii.):

"The original author alone could say with confidence that he meant '*rivers*,' which thenceforward became the traditional and admitted explanation, and is, accordingly, so supplied by the scholiast."

In the following passage (p. xxv.), however, Prof. Wilson admits that it is doubtful whether these explanations had always actually come down from the age of the authors of the hymns :—

"How far his" (*i.e.* the author's) "lecture and amplification may have been preserved uncorrupted through successive generations, until they reached Yâska, and eventually Sâyaṇa, may be reasonably liable to question; but that the explanations of these scholiasts were not arbitrary, but were such as had been established by the practice of preceding schools, and were generally current at their several eras, can admit of no doubt. Even if it were not so, their undeniable learning and their sympathy with the views and feelings of their countrymen, amongst whom were the original authors and expounders of the Sûktas, must give a weight to their authority which no European scholar, however profound his knowledge of Sanskrit or of the Vedas, can, in my opinion, be entitled to claim."

The following is Prof. Rudolph Roth's explanation of the system which he has pursued in the interpretation of Vedic words in the great Sanskrit and German Lexicon published by himself and Dr. Boehtlingk. I translate from the preface to the first vol. of the Lexicon published in 1855 :

"As the aids furnished to us by recent authors for the understanding of the Vedic texts are but scanty, we are the more dependent on the contributions made to their interpretation by Indian scholarship itself, *i.e.*, on the commentaries. And, in fact, so far as regards one of the branches of Vedic literature, the treatises on theology and worship, we can desire no better guides than these commentators, so exact in all respects, who follow their texts word by word, who, so long as even the semblance of a misconception might arise, are never weary of repeating what they have frequently said before, and who often appear as if they had been writing for us foreigners rather than for their own priestly alumni who had grown up in the midst of these conceptions and impressions. Here, where their task is to explain the widely-ramified, ingenious, and often far-fetched symbolism of their ceremonial, to elucidate the numberless minutiæ on the observance of which in religious worship, eternal salvation or perdition depends, they are on their proper ground. For in the Brâhmaṇas there breathes the same spirit which works downward through the whole course of orthodox Indian theology, and in particular has pervaded those Brahmanical schools which some centuries ago were so zealously engaged in investigating and explaining the most prominent treatises of their ancient theological literature.

"The case, however, is quite different when the same men assume the task of interpreting the ancient collections of hymns. These texts are not the creations of theological speculation, nor have they sprung out of the soil of that rigidly prescribed, minute, liturgical ceremonial to which we have alluded, but they are for the most part productions of the oldest religious-lyrical poetry, the artistic cultivation of which was as little confined to particular families or castes as was the offering of daily sacrifice and prayer: in them a world of deities lives, and a worship is mirrored, which are essentially distinct from the system taught in the Brâhmaṇas; they speak a language divided from that of the Brâhmanas (which scarcely differs from the so-called classical Sanskrit) by a chasm as wide as that which separates the Latin of the Salic hymns from that of M. Terentius Varro. Here, therefore, there were required not only quite different qualifications for interpretation, but also a freedom of judgment and a greater breadth of view and of historical intuitions. Freedom of judgment, however, was wanting to priestly learning among all the nations of heathen antiquity, whilst in India no one has ever had any conception of historical development.

"Thus the very qualities which have made those commentators excellent guides to an understanding of the theological treatises, render them unsuitable conductors on that far older and quite differently circumstanced domain. As the so-called classical Sanskrit was perfectly familiar to them, they sought its ordinary idiom in the Vedic hymns also. Since any difference in the ritual appeared to them inconceivable, and the present forms were believed to have existed from the beginning of the world, they fancied that the patriarchs of the Indian religion must have sacrificed in the very same manner. As the recognized mythological and cosmical systems of their own age appeared to them unassailable and revealed verities, they must necessarily (so the commentators thought) be discoverable in that centre-point of revelation, the hymns of the ancient Rishis, who had, indeed, lived in familiar intercourse with the gods, and possessed far higher wisdom than the succeeding generations.

"It is unnecessary to enlarge on this state of things, or to illustrate it by examples.[1] Nor will it be expected that we should here indicate at length the very considerable advantage which is derivable from the works of these interpreters, in spite of all their imperfections. The whole state of the case is neither difficult to recognise, nor singular in its kind. The sacred books of the ancient nations were, as a general rule, explained in the same manner by later generations according to the prevailing systems of theology and the higher or lower state of science; and in every case this interpretation was given out as being a tradition, that is, it claimed for itself an antiquity and a dignity of which it could not always boast with truth. Besides, to give an example, it has never occurred to any one to make our understanding of the Hebrew books of the Old Testament depend on the Talmud and the Rabbins, while there are

[1] [Though Prof. Roth does not consider it necessary to give instances in proof of his assertions, I may allude to the way in which Sâyaṇa considers the dwarf-incarnation of Vishṇu to be referred to in R.V. i. 22 16 ff., and identifies the Rudra of the hymns with the husband of Pârvatî; see his note on R.V. i. 114, 6; and Sanskrit Texts, iv. 57 and 257. Yâska, however, and the older authors referred to by him, Nir. xii 19, seem to know, or, at least, they say, nothing of the dwarf-incarnation.—J.M.]

not wanting scholars who hold it as the duty of a conscientious interpreter of the Veda to translate in conformity with Sâyaṇa, Mahîdhara, etc. Consequently, we do not believe, like H. H. Wilson, that Sâyaṇa, for instance, understood the expressions of the Veda better than any European interpreter; but we think that a conscientious European interpreter may understand the Veda far better and more correctly than Sâyaṇa. We do not esteem it our first task to arrive at that understanding of the Veda which was current in India some centuries ago, but to search out the sense which the poets themselves have put into their hymns and utterances. Hence we are of opinion that the writings of Sâyaṇa and the other commentators do not form a rule for the interpreter, but are merely one of those helps of which the latter will avail himself for the execution of his undoubtedly difficult task, a task which is not to be accomplished at the first onset, or by any single individual. . . . . .

"We have, therefore, endeavoured to follow the path prescribed by philology, to derive from the texts themselves the sense which they contain, by a juxtaposition of all the passages which are cognate in diction or contents;—a tedious and laborious path, in which neither the commentators nor the translators have preceded us. The double duty of exegete and lexicographer has thus devolved upon us. A simply etymological procedure, practised as it must be by those who seek to divine the sense of a word from the sole consideration of the passage before them, without regard to the ten or twenty other passages in which it recurs, cannot possibly lead to a correct result. Such a procedure, even if practised in conformity with philological principles, moves in far too wide logical circles to admit of its always hitting the right point, and gives rise to conceptions which are far too general and colourless, which, perhaps, indeed, include within them the firmly defined and sharply stamped meaning which the word contains, but fail to reproduce it in its peculiarity, and therefore in its power and beauty.

"Of this nature is the procedure which the commentators have adopted, and whereby they clearly demonstrate that they have not simultaneously mastered the entire vocabulary of these books, and at the same time that they have not handled the individual passages according to any fixed traditional interpretation. Hence it happens that they have assigned to a large number of nouns in the Veda the sense of *power*, *sacrifice*, *food*, *wisdom*, etc., and to many verbs, that of *going*,[1] *moving*, etc., when all these words are distinct from one

[1] [The Nighaṇṭu ii., 14, contains no less than 122 verbs, to which the sense of *going* is assigned.—J.M.]

another, have a definite value and a clear significance of their own, and in many cases have scarcely the most distant connection with those general conceptions. And it is only by the reinstatement of these misapprehended words in their lost rights that the Veda acquires a striking meaning, force, and richness of expression, and gives us an entirely different image of the world of thought in the earliest antiquity.

"No one who knows the difficulties of such an occupation will refuse us indulgence for our undoubtedly numerous mistakes, mistakes which, in the progress of the work, will become first and most distinctly manifest to ourselves."

I have considered it proper to give this long extract from the preface to the St. Petersburg Lexicon, as though Prof. Roth is by no means the sole representative of the school of interpretation which he here defends, he has, by the compilation of the large portion of his Dictionary which has already appeared, done far more than any other Sanskritist has yet accomplished to carry his principles into practice.

Before adverting to the criticism which this passage has received from Prof. Goldstücker, I shall make a short quotation from Prof. Max Müller's preface to the 3rd vol. of his Rig-veda, which must be understood as laying down principles of interpretation similar to those which are advocated by Roth. After remarking that "the conviction seems to be growing more and more general, that without this (Sâyaṇa's) Commentary an accurate and scholarlike knowledge of the Veda could never have been obtained;" Müller goes on to say:—

"It would have been equally wrong, however, to consider Sâyaṇa's commentary as an infallible authority with regard to the interpretation of the Veda. Sâyaṇa gives the traditional, but not the original, sense of the Vaidik hymns. . . . If, therefore, we wish to know how the Brahmans, from the time of the composition of the first Brâhmaṇa to the present day, understood and interpreted the hymns of their ancient Rishis, we ought to translate them in strict accordance with Sâyaṇa's gloss. . . . . Nor could it be said that the tradition of the Brahmans, which Sâyaṇa embodied in his work, after the lapse of at least three thousand years, had changed the whole character of the Rig-veda. By far the greater part of these hymns is so simple and straightforward, that there can be no doubt that their original meaning was exactly the same as their traditional interpretation. But no religion, no poetry, no law, no language can resist the tear and wear of thirty centuries; and in the Veda, as in other works, handed down to us from a very remote antiquity, the sharp edges of primitive thought, the delicate features of a young language, the fresh hue of unconscious poetry, have been washed away by the successive waves of what we call *tradition*, whether we look upon it as a principle of growth or decay. To restore the primitive outlines of the Vaidik period of thought will be a work of great difficulty." pp. vii., f. He then goes on to quote a passage from a previous essay of his own, in which, after laying it down as a rule that, "not a corner of the Brâhmaṇas, the Sûtras, Yâska, and Sâyaṇa should be left unexplored before we venture to propose a rendering of our own," he, a little further on, proceeds thus: "To make such misunderstandings" (as are found in the Brâhmaṇas) "possible, we must assume a considerable interval between the composition of the hymns and the Brâhmaṇas. As the authors of the Brâhmaṇas were blinded by theology, the authors of the still later Niruktas were deceived by etymological fictions, and both conspired to mislead by their authority later and more sensible commentators, such as Sâyaṇa. Where Sâyaṇa has no authority to mislead him, his Commentary is at all events rational; but still his scholastic notions would never allow him to accept the free interpretation which a comparative study of these venerable documents forces upon the unprejudiced scholar. We must therefore discover ourselves the real vestiges of these ancient poets," etc.

I now come to Prof. Goldstücker's strictures (Pâṇini, pp. 241 ff.) on the principles of Vedic interpretation laid down by Prof. Roth. He thus expresses his opinion of the value, and of the method, of the Indian commentators:—

"Without the vast information these commentators have disclosed to us,—without their method of explaining the obscurest texts,—in one word, without their scholarship, we should still stand at the outer doors of Hindu antiquity. . . . The whole religious life of ancient India is based on tradition. . . . Tradition tells us, through the voice of the commentators, who re-echo the voice of their ancestors, how the nation, from immemorial times, understood the sacred texts, what inferences they drew from them, what influence they allowed them to exercise on their religious, philosophical, ethical,—in a word, on their national, development. . . . But it would be utterly erroneous to assume that a scholar like Sâyaṇa, or even a copy of him, like Mahîdhara, contented himself with being the mouthpiece of his predecessors or ancestors. They not only record the sense of the Vaidik texts and the sense of the words of which these texts consist, but they endeavour to show that the interpretations which they give are *consistent with the grammatical requirements of the language itself*."

Prof. Goldstücker then quotes (pp. 245 f.) a portion of the remarks of Prof. Roth which I have cited above, and proceeds to controvert a statement, which he ascribes to that scholar, that Sâyaṇa and the other commentators give us "only that sense of the Veda which was current in India some centuries ago:"—

"A bolder statement," writes Prof. Goldstücker (p. 248), "I defy any scholar to have met with in any book. Sâyana incessantly refers to Yâska. All his explanations show that he stands on the ground of the *oldest legends and traditions*,—of such traditions, moreover, as have no connection whatever with the creeds of those sects which represent the degenerated Hindu faith of his time."

Prof. Goldstücker then goes on (pp. 248 ff.) to argue that Prof. Roth, from imperfect acquaintance with the labours of the Indian commentators, is not entitled to depreciate their qualifications for the correct interpretation of the Veda, or to assert the superior fitness of European scholars for this task; rejects as absurd the idea of the former not being able, as well as the latter, to bring together and compare all the passages in which particular words occur; maintains that in the case of those words which occur but once in the Veda, and in regard to which, therefore, no comparison with other passages is possible, the guesses of Sâyaṇa are as good as those of his critic; reiterates his opinion that Sâyaṇa's method of procedure was not purely etymological, but involved a reference to tradition; and ridicules the assertion that a European scholar can understand the Veda more correctly than Sâyaṇa, or arrive more nearly at the meaning which the Rishis gave to their own hymns.

With reference to the strictures of Prof. Goldstücker on the assertion which he attributes to Prof. Roth, that Sâyaṇa and the other later commentators give "*only* that sense of the Veda which was current in India some centuries ago,"

I would remark that I find nothing in the passage quoted by Prof. Goldstücker, and by myself, from Roth, to show that the latter scholar, although he refuses to be bound by the interpretations of the mediæval scholiasts, and may regard these interpretations as having been in great part initiated by those scholiasts themselves, is therefore disposed to deny that they may in part have been founded on older materials handed down by former generations. Because a body of interpretation is spoken of as *existing* at a particular date, it does not follow that no part of it is admitted to have had an earlier origin. In fact, Prof. Roth cannot for a moment be imagined to have ignored the assistance which Sâyaṇa had derived from the older work of Yâska, the Nirukta, a book of which he himself had, only three years before the preface to his Dictionary was written, published an edition. From the concluding pages of that work (which appeared in 1852), I translate the following additional observations on the Indian commentators, which shew that in Roth's opinion Yâska, though much more ancient, and otherwise more advantageously situated, than Sâyaṇa, stood yet essentially on the same footing with the latter, being rather a learned exegete, working, in all cases of difficulty, by an etymological process, than the depositary of any certain interpretation of the hymns handed down by tradition from the period when they were intelligible to every one who recited them :—

"In regard to the point how much or how little the Indian commentators from Yâska downwards contribute to the understanding of the Veda, a more correct judgment than that hitherto current will be formed as soon as some of them shall have become completely known. The interpretation of the Veda can lay upon itself no heavier fetters than by believing in the infallibility of these guides, or in the existence of a valuable tradition supposed to have been enjoyed by them. A superficial observation has already shown that their mode of interpretation is simply the reverse of a traditional one, that it is in fact a grammatical and etymological one, which has only so much in common with the traditional method, that it explains each verse, each line, each word by itself, without enquiring how far the results so obtained agree with those derived from other quarters.

"If any person is disposed to find tradition in the fact that the commentators coincide in having in their minds one tolerably simple scheme of conception, *e.g.*, in regard to the functions of a particular god, or even in regard to the entire contents of the hymns, which they unceasingly force into the texts, he may indeed call that tradition, but he will at the same time admit that this poverty of intuition is nothing which we should very much covet. This scheme embraces the scholastic conceptions, which had become fixed at an early period, but yet not before the date when the Vedic hymns had already become the object of a purely learned study, and when the religious ideas and social circumstances on which they are based had for a long time lost their vitality. In spite of all the irregularities of their imaginative faculty, the Indians have at all times had a longing for arrangement, classification, systematizing, and have through these, in themselves praiseworthy, tendencies very frequently given rise to the greatest confusion. The Vedic literature, too, affords numerous proofs of this.

"The same remarks apply, in all essential points, to Yâska, as to Sâyaṇa, or any other of the later writers. Yâska, too, is a learned interpreter, who works with the materials which science had collected before his age; but he has a prodigious advantage in point of time before those compilers of detailed, continuous commentaries, and belongs to a quite different literary period, when Sanskrit still existed in a process of natural growth. And his work gains for us a greater importance from the fact that it is indeed the only one of its kind which has been preserved. Even those commentators who lived five centuries and more before us know of no other comparable to it in rank and antiquity, and are consequently unwearied in their appeals to Yâska's authority. The half of the Nirukta might be restored out of Sâyaṇa's Commentary on the Rig-veda."

Prof. Roth then goes on to give some account of the different schools of interpretation, as well as the names of individual teachers, anterior to Yâska (pp. 220 ff.).

I will add here the opinion of one other eminent scholar, Prof. Benfey, on the points at issue between Profs. Roth and Goldstücker. I quote at second hand from the Gött. Gel. Anz. 1858, p. 1608 f., as extracted by Prof. Weber at the end of his reply to Prof. Goldstücker's Pâṇini, in the Indische Studien, v. 174 f. :—

"Every one who has carefully studied the Indian interpretations is aware that absolutely no continuous tradition, extending from the composition of the Vedas to their explanation by Indian scholars, can be assumed; that, on the contrary, between the genuine poetic remains of Vedic antiquity and their interpretations a long-continued break in tradition must have intervened, out of which at most the comprehension of some particulars may have been rescued and handed down to later times by means of liturgical usages and words, formulæ, and perhaps, also, poems connected therewith. Besides these remains of tradition, which must be estimated as very scanty, the interpreters of the Veda had, in the main, scarcely any other helps than those which, for the most part, are still at our command, the usage of the classical speech, and the grammatical and etymological-lexicographical investigation of words. At the utmost, they found some aid in materials preserved in local dialects; but this advantage is almost entirely outweighed by the comparison which we are able to institute with the Zend, and that which we can make (though here we must of course proceed with caution and prudence) with the other languages cognate to the Sanskrit,—a comparison which has already supplied so many helps to a clearer understanding of the Vedas. But quite irrespectively of all particular aids, the Indian method of interpretation becomes in its whole essence an entirely false one, owing to the prejudice with which it chooses to conceive the ancient circumstances and ideas which have become quite strange to it, from its own religious stand-point, so many centuries more recent; whilst, on the other hand, an advantage for the comprehension of the whole is secured to us by the acquaintance (drawn from analogous relations) with the life, the conceptions, the wants, of ancient peoples and popular songs, which we possess,—an advantage which, even if the Indians owed more details than they actually do owe, to tradition, would not be eclipsed by their interpretation."

It appears, therefore, that the views of Prof. Roth, in regard to the proper principles of Vedic interpretation, are shared by Professors Müller, Weber, and Benfey; whilst even my learned friend, Prof. Goldstücker himself, cannot be altogether acquitted (as I shall hereafter show) of a certain heretical tendency to deviate in practice from the interpretations of Sâyaṇa,—a tendency which may, perhaps, as his Dictionary advances, become by and by developed into a more pronounced heterodoxy.

I now proceed to inquire, in some detail, whether any considerable traces exist in ancient Indian literature of a tradition of the sense of the Vedic hymns handed continuously down from the earliest period. If any such traces are extant, they must be found primarily in the Brâhmaṇas, or the Âraṇyakas, or in Yâska. Do these works then contain any interpretations, at once positive and satisfactory, of any considerable portion of the hymns? I begin with the oldest works,—the Brâhmaṇas. In a quotation which I have made above from Prof. Max Müller, he states his opinion that "we must assume a considerable interval between the composition of the hymns and the Brâhmaṇas." There is no doubt that this is true. The language and the contents of these two classes of works are alike widely different. Referring to the same author's "History of Ancient Indian Literature" for a complete account of the Brâhmaṇas, I will merely quote from it a few sentences, to show how little in his estimation these books are likely to aid us in understanding the hymns:—

"There is throughout the Brâhmaṇas," he writes, p. 432, "such a complete misunderstanding of the original intention of the Vedic hymns, that we can hardly understand how such an estrangement could have taken place, unless there had been at some time or other a sudden and violent break in the chain of tradition. The authors of the Brâhmaṇas evidently imagined that those ancient hymns were written simply for the sake of their sacrifices, and whatever interpretation they thought fit to assign to those acts, the same, they supposed, had to be borne out by the hymns. This idea has vitiated the whole system of Indian exegesis. . . . . . Not only was the true nature of the gods, as conceived by the early poets, completely lost sight of, but new gods were actually created out of words which were never intended to be names of divine beings."

Müller goes on, p. 433, to illustrate this by referring to the fact that a god, Ka (Who), was invented out of certain interrogative verses of the Rig-veda in which the worshipper asks to *whom* he shall address his worship. Thus, for example, the Ṣatapatha Brâhmaṇa, vii. 4, 1, 19, after quoting the first verse of R.V. x. 121, ending with "to what god shall we offer our oblation?" says, "Ka (Who) is Prajâpati; to him let us offer our oblation."[1] Müller then refers to the taste-

[1] Compare "Sanskrit Texts," iv. 13, note.

less explanation given in a Brâhmaṇa of the epithet "golden-handed" applied to the Sun in the hymns, that the Sun had lost his hand, and had got instead one of gold.[1] The Ṣatapatha Brâhmaṇa, xiii. 6, 1, 2, understands, very improbably, the Virâj alluded to in Rig-veda, x. 90, 5 ("From him (Purusha) was born Virâj, and from Virâj, Purusha"), to be the metre of that name, and declares that Purusha, the sacrifice, was begotten by Purusha on Virâj. Again, Rig-veda, x. 61, 7, which apparently refers in a figurative manner to some atmospheric phenomenon, is explained in Ṣatapatha Brâhmaṇa, i. 7, 4, 1, as referring to a legend about Prajâpati having literally had sexual intercourse with his own daughter, so as to occasion scandal and indignation among the gods. The same Brâhmaṇa contains (xi. 5, 1, 1 ff.) the legend of Purûravas and Urvaṣî, in the course of which five verses of the 95th hymn of the 10th book of the R.V. are introduced as part of the conversation which passed between the hero and the nymph, but it does not give any detailed explanation of these verses, and it does not quote at all the verses which make up the rest of the hymn, and which are generally far more difficult to interpret. Again, in the Aitareya Brâhmaṇa vii. 13-18, where the story of Ṣunaḥṣepa is told, a large number of verses, composing the 24th to the 30th hymns of the first book of the R.V., and a few from the fourth and fifth books, are referred to as having been uttered by the hero of the legend, but are not even quoted at length, much less explained. (See Dr. Haug's Ait. Br., vol. ii. pp. 466 ff.) There is indeed in Ait. Br. viii. 26 (see Haug, vol. ii. pp. 530 ff.) an interpretation given of three verses of R.V. iv. 50 (vv. 7-9), but this, whatever its value otherwise may be, is but an inconsiderable contribution to the exposition of the hymns. Ṣ. P. Br. x. 5, 3, 1, contains a paraphrase of R.V. x. 129, 1, which is not without value. (See my former article on the "Progress of the Vedic Religion," p. 346 f.) Some explanation of R.V. i. 25, 10, also is given in Ṣ. P. Br. v. 4, 4, 5. But as far as I have looked into the Brâhmaṇas,

[1] See "Contributions to a Knowledge of Vedic Theogony," etc. in this Journal, for 1864, p. 116, note.

I have seen but very little which can be of much service in throwing light on the original sense of the hymns.

I observe, indeed, that Professor Müller thus expresses himself (Anc. Sansk. Lit., p. 153) in regard to the use which he thinks may be made of the Brâhmaṇas, etc., for the purpose referred to:—

"For explanations of old Vedic words, for etymologies and synonymous expressions, the Brâhmaṇas contain very rich materials. . . . . Whole verses and hymns are shortly explained there; and the Âraṇyakas and Upanishads, if included, would furnish richer sources for Vedic etymologies than even the Nirukta itself. The beginning of the Aitareya Âraṇyaka is in fact a commentary on the beginning of the Rig-veda; and if all the passages of the Brâhmaṇas were collected where one word is explained by another with which it is joined merely by the particle *vai*,[1] they would even now give a rich harvest for a new Nirukta."

This passage, however, must be taken in connection with those which have been quoted above from the same writer. I am unable to refer to the Aitareya Âraṇyaka to which he alludes. But judging from the views which he has expressed elsewhere, I conclude that he does not expect, as the result of the researches which he recommends (even if pushed to the utmost extent) into all the existing remains of Indian literature exterior to the hymns themselves, any very extensive or material assistance towards the restoration of the original sense of the latter. But whatever might be the issue of the course of investigation thus suggested, it is at least presupposed in Prof. Müller's recommendation that this process of carefully searching the Brâhmaṇas and Âraṇyakas for interpretations of obsolete Vedic words and phrases has not yet been pursued to a sufficient extent by any of the Indian etymologists or commentators. But if this be true—if any considerable amount of important materials suitable to their purpose has been neglected by Yâska or Sâyaṇa—it is clear that we cannot look to either of those writers as our final or sufficient authority.

[1] [As, for instance, in the cases *viṣo vai pastyâḥ* (Ṣ. P. Br. v. 4, 4, 5) *Prajâpatir vai Kaḥ*, Ṣ. P. Br. vii. 4, 1, 19.—J.M].

I now come to the Nighaṇṭus, and the Nirukta of Yâska. The Nighaṇṭus[1] form a vocabulary of terms, many of which are obsolete. The first three sections are almost entirely made up of lists of so-called synonymes, varying in number from two to one hundred and twenty-two, of nouns or verbs of well-known signification, such as *pṛthivî*, "earth," *hiraṇya*, "gold," *antariksha*, "atmosphere," *jval*, "to burn," *gam*, "to go." The remaining two sections consist of mere lists of words of different significations, which are left unexplained. There does not seem to be any reason to doubt that in the first three sections of this work the general sense of many obsolete words has been preserved by tradition; though as the terms declared to be synonymous are often very numerous, it is clear from the nature of the case, as Prof. Roth observes (see above), that the specific sense, and particular shade of meaning, represented by each, must be often left in the dark. And an examination of the lists puts this beyond a doubt. Thus under the synonymes of *vâch*, "speech," we find such words as *ṣloka*, *nivid*, *ṛk*, *gâthâ*, *anushṭup*, words denoting different kinds of verses or compositions, which can never have been employed as simple equivalents of speech in the abstract. The value of these lists therefore for the purpose of defining the precise signification of words is very limited. And even if the first three sections were of more value than they are in this respect, they are far from embracing the whole of the difficult words in the Veda. The fourth section contains two hundred and seventy-eight words which are not explained at all, though there are, no doubt, a good many among them which do not require any explanation, as their sense is notorious. The Nirukta of Yâska is a sort of commentary on the Nighaṇṭus. It begins with these words: "A record has been composed, which we have to explain. It is called the Nighaṇṭus." The introduction to the work (i. 1—ii. 4) contains the outlines of a grammatical system, and an ex-

[1] Prof. Roth considers this vocabulary to be older than Yâska. (Introduction to Nirukta, p. xii. f.). Müller, too, (Anc. Ind. Lit. 154), says, "probably these lists existed in his family long before his time."

planation of the advantages, objects, principles and methods of exegesis. This is followed (ii. 5—iii. 22) by remarks suggested by the lists of explained synonymes composing the first three sections of the Nighaṇṭus. In the succeeding chapters (iv.—vi.) of the Nirukta, the unexplained terms in the fourth section of the Nighaṇṭus are interpreted; whilst in the last six books the list of words, chiefly names of deities, contained in the fifth section of the Nighaṇṭus, is elucidated.[1] The thirteenth and fourteenth chapters, styled Nirukta-pariṣishṭa, appear to be the work of a later writer.

The Nirukta makes frequent reference to the Brâhmaṇas, adduces various legends, such as those about Devâpi (xi. 10) and Viṣvâmitra (ii. 24), and also alludes to various schools of Vedic interpretation which existed anterior to the time of its author, such as the Nairuktas or etymologists, the Aitihâsikas or legendary writers, and the Yâjnikas or ritualists.[2] In the course of his work, Yâska supplies some specimens of the mode of explaining the hymns adopted by these different classes of expositors, from which it would appear that each school interpreted from its own special point of view, and according to its own literary, moral, or professional tendencies and prepossessions. Thus we are told (Nirukta, xi. 29 and 31) that the Nairuktas understood Anumati, Râkâ, Sinîvâlî, and Kuhû to be goddesses, while the Yâjnikas took them for the new and full moons. On one point the greatest diversity of opinion prevailed. The gods called Aṣvins were a great enigma. The Nirukta (xii. 1) gives the following answers to the question who they were: "'Heaven and Earth,' say some; 'Day and Night,' say others; 'the Sun and Moon,' say others; 'two kings, performers of the holy acts,' say the Aitihâsikas."[3] In his explanation of R.V. i. 164, 32, Yâska

[1] See all this more fully stated in Roth's Illustrations of the Nirukta, p. 3.

[2] See Roth's Illustrations of the Nirukta, pp. 220 ff.

[3] Sâyaṇa also mentions some of these different schools of interpreters in different parts of his commentary. Thus on R.V. i. 64, 8, he says: *Pṛshatyaḥ*, the Maruts' instruments of conveyance, are does marked with white spots according to the Aitihâsikas, and a line of variously coloured clouds according to the Nairuktas." Again, he tells us that writers of the former class understood R.V. i. 174, 2, of the cities belonging to Vṛttra's Asuras, whilst those of the latter class

(ii. 8) refers to the Parivrâjakas (ascetic mendicants) as attributing one sense to the close of that verse, while the Nairuktas assigned a different one.[1] It is thus clear that from the earliest period there were diversities of opinion in regard to the sense of the hymns. As we come down to later times, when speculation had been further developed, we find some new varieties of interpretation. Thus in the Nirukta-pariṣishṭa, i. 9, the "four defined grades or stages of speech" referred to in R.V. i. 164, 45, are said to be diversely explained, "by the Rishis as meaning the four mystic words *om, bhûḥ, bhuvaḥ, svar;* by the grammarians as denoting nouns, verbs, prepositions, and particles; by the ritualists as referring to the hymns, the liturgical precepts, the Brâhmaṇas, and the ordinary language; by the etymologists as designating the Ṛik, the Yajush, the Sâman texts, and the current language; whilst by others they are thought to signify the languages of serpents, birds, reptiles, and the vernacular; and the spiritualists (*âtmapravâdâḥ*) understand them of the modes of speech in beasts, musical instruments (?), wild animals, and soul."

Yâska gives also the names of no less than seventeen interpreters who had preceded him,[2] and whose explanations of the Veda are often conflicting. Thus we are informed (Nir. iii. 8) that some understood the "five peoples" (*panchajanâḥ*) mentioned in R.V. x. 53, 4, to be the Gandharvas, Pitris, gods, Asuras, and Rakshases; whilst Aupamanyana took them for the four castes and the Nishâdas.[3] From Nir. iv. 3, it appears that while Yâska himself understood the word *ṣitâma* which occurs

understood it of the clouds. In like manner, on viii. 66, 10, he gives us two separate interpretations of that verse, the first that of the Nairuktas, who expounded it of natural phenomena, of showers brought by the sun (represented by Vishṇu), and the second that of the Aitihâsikas, who explained it mythologically in conformity with a story drawn from the Brâhmaṇa of the Charakas.

[1] The ascetics, influenced, perhaps, by their own feelings of estrangement from family life, gave to the words in question the meaning "The father of many children suffers distress." The Etymologists understood the same clause of the fructifying effects of rain.

[2] Roth, Illustrations, pp. 221 f.

[3] In Nir. iii. 15, several different derivations of the word *vidhavâ*, "widow," are given. It is said to be either = *vidhâtṛkâ*, "without a supporter;" or, according to Charmaṣiras (one of Yâska's predecessors), to come from *vidhavana* or *vidhâvana;* or to be derived from *vi* + *dhava*, "without a man."

in the Vâjasaneyi Sanhitâ, xxi. 43, of the *shoulder* of the sacrificial victim, Ṣâkapûṇi took it for the *female organ*, Taiṭîki for the *liver*, and Gâlava for the *fat*. Again, Nir. vi. 13, tells us that Aurṇabhâva understood the word *Nâsatyau* (an epithet of the Aṣvins) to mean "true, not false" (*satyau, na asatyau*; Âgrâyaṇa took it to mean "leaders of truth" *satyasya praṇetârau*); whilst Yâska himself suggests that it may signify "nose-born" *nâsikâ-prabhavau*). From Nir. vii. 23, it appears that whilst the early ritualists held the deity lauded in R.V. i. 59, 6, to be the Sun, Ṣâkapûṇi on the contrary held that it was Agni Vaiṣvânara. Further, in Nir. viii. 2, we are informed that Kraushṭuki held Draviṇodas to mean Indra, but Ṣâkapûṇi considered the term to denote Agni. Kâtthakya was of opinion that the word *idhma* signified merely the wood employed in sacrifice, while Ṣâkapûṇi thought it stood for Agni (Nir. viii. 4, 5). So, again, Kâtthakya understood Narâṣansa to designate "sacrifice," but Ṣâkapûṇi took it for a name of Agni (*ibid.* 6); Kâtthakya explained the "divine doors" (R.V. x. 110, 5), of the house-doors at sacrifice, but Ṣâkapûṇi took them to stand for Agni (*ibid.* 10); the former interpreter held Vanaspati to be the sacrificial post, but Ṣâkapûṇi asserted that it was a name of Agni (*ibid.* 17). In like manner, Yâska's predecessors were not agreed as to what was meant by Vishṇu's three steps mentioned in R.V. i. 22, 17, Ṣâkapûṇi maintaining that they were planted on the earth, the atmosphere, and the sky respectively; and Aurṇabhâva that it was the hill over which the sun rises, the meridian, and the hill where he sets, that were the localities referred to. Finally, the etymologists declared that the word *Sâdhyas* in R.V. x. 90, 16, denoted the gods residing in the sky, whilst according to a legend (*âkhyâna*) it represented a former age of the gods (*pûrvaṃ deva-yugam*: comp. R.V. x. 72, 2, 3).

There was one of Yâska's predecessors who had actually the audacity to assert that the science of Vedic exposition was useless, as the Vedic hymns and formulæ were obscure, unmeaning, or mutually contradictory. As instances of obscurity, he cites the texts in which the words *amyak* (R.V.

i. 169, 3), *yâdṛṣmin* (R.V. v. 44, 8), *jârayâyi* (R.V. vi. 12, 4), and *kâṇukâ* (R.V. viii. 66, 4), occur. In regard to this charge of obscurity, Yâska replies that it is not the fault of the post that the blind man does not see it; it is the man's fault.[1] It would appear from the objections of this rationalist, that in his day many learned men had great difficulties in regard to the sense of different passages of the hymns. It is true indeed that Durgâchârya, the commentator on the Nirukta, seems to consider Kautsa a mere man of straw, into whose mouth these objections are dramatically put for the sake of their being refuted;[2] but I do not see why Kautsa should be regarded as a fictitious personage any more than any of the other predecessors of Yâska who are named in the Nirukta. And even if he were admitted to be so, it may be assumed as certain that Yâska, an orthodox believer, would never have alluded to sceptical doubts of this description unless they had been previously started by some of his predecessors, and had been commonly current in his time. We shall see further on how he succeeds in the attempt he makes to explain some of the texts which Kautsa charges with obscurity.

The question how far Yâska can be regarded as the depositary of a real and satisfactory Vedic tradition has been thus already, in part, answered, and in an unfavourable sense, by the account I have given of the differences of opinion existing among his predecessors. I now proceed to enquire further how far his own language and method of interpretation show him to have been walking in the clear light of day, or groping in the dark, and merely guessing at the sense of the hymns.

It is extremely unlikely that, with all the appliances which it appears he had at his command in the works of his predecessors, which he quotes, and probably others besides, Yâska should not have been able to determine the sense of many words which later scholars like Sâyaṇa had no means of dis-

[1] See Nirukta, i. 15 f.; Roth's Illustrations, pp. 11 f.; and "Sanskrit Texts," ii. 181 ff.

[2] "Sanskrit Texts," ii. 184.

covering. According to Prof. Max Müller,[1] Yâska lived in the fourth century before our era. Prof. Goldstücker holds that he was anterior to Pâṇini, whose date he considers to be involved in impenetrable obscurity, and yet, he thinks, must have been anterior to that of Buddha, whose death again he speaks of as the remotest date of Hindu antiquity which can be called a real date,[2] agreeing apparently with Lassen in placing it in 543 B.C.,[3] whilst Müller refers it to 477 B.C. Yâska was thus some two thousand years older than Sâyaṇa. We may therefore often assume, that when he affirms positively that a word unknown to later Sanskrit has such and such a meaning, even though he attaches to it an etymology, and when the sense suits the passage, he had grounds for his assertion. Thus, when he says (iv. 15) that *tugvan* means a "ford," or (v. 22) *ṣvaghnin*, a "gambler," or (vi. 26) that *bekanâṭa* signifies a "usurer," there is no reason to dispute his affirmation. But whenever he seems to draw the meaning from the etymology, and his interpretation does not yield a good sense, we must doubt whether his opinion rested on any trustworthy tradition. And again, when he gives two or more alternative or optional explanations of the same word, all apparently founded on mere etymology, we are justified in supposing that he had no earlier authority for his guide, and that his renderings are simply conjectural. Many instances, I believe, can be given where the phenomenon last described occurs; and I shall proceed to bring forward some specimens. There are also cases in which Yâska is positive as to the meaning he assigns, but in which the sense of the passage, or a collation of other texts, justifies us in departing from his rendering. In all these passages I shall at the same time give the interpretation proposed by Sâyaṇa, if it be within my reach. And as it will sometimes be found that Sâyaṇa departs from Yâska, we shall, in such instances, either have to conclude that the older interpreter is wrong—in which event ancient tradition must in that particular instance

[1] "Last Results of Sanskrit Researches" in "Bunsen's Christianity and Mankind," vol. iii. p. 137.

[2] Pâṇini, pp. 225, 227.

[3] *Ibid*, pp. 231, 232.

be of no value—or that Sâyaṇa does not there follow tradition at all. In such cases either the value of the supposed tradition, or its faithful reproduction by the later commentator, will be disproved.

The following are specimens of these different cases, together with some instances of words which do not occur in the Nirukta, but in which Sâyaṇa gives a variety of inconsistent explanations :—

1. *Atharyu* is an epithet of Agni. Yâska (v. 10) renders it by *atanavantam,* "going" or "moving." Sâyaṇa, in R.V. vii. 1, 1, explains it by *âgamyam atanavantaṃ vâ, i.e.,* either "to be gone to, approached," or "going," "moving."[1] It thus appears that he does not implicitly follow Yâska, and was not sure of the sense. Prof. Goldstücker, *s.v.*, renders it "moving constantly." Prof. Roth, *s.v.*, thinks it means "having sharp points like a lance."

2. *Anânuda* is an adjective not found in the Nirukta, but in different passages of the R.V. On i. 53, 8, Sâyaṇa explains it as *anuchara-rahitaḥ,* "without followers ;" on ii. 21, 4, and ii. 23, 11, as "one after whom no other gives," *i.e.,* "unequalled in giving." On this Prof. Goldstücker remarks: "Both meanings of the word, as given according to the Comm., seem doubtful ;" but he proposes no other. Roth, *s.v.*, translates it by "unyielding."

(1) *Anushvadham,* (2) *anu svadhâm,* (3) *svadhâm anu,* (4) *svadhayâ,* (5) *svadhâbhiḥ,* (6) *svadhâvat.* The first of these words occurs in various texts of the R.V., one of which, iii. 47, 1, is quoted in Nir. iv. 8, where the word is explained by *anv annam,* "after food." Prof. Goldstücker, *s.v.*, explains it thus: 1, "in consequence of (partaking of) food, through food, viz., soma, etc. ; 2, food for food, to every food (as clarified butter) ; 3, after every oblation." The sixth word, *svadhâvat,* occurs in two places in the Nirukta, viz., in x. 6 (where R.V. vii. 46, 1, is quoted), when it is an epithet, in the dative, of Rudra ; and in xii. 17 (where R.V. vi. 58, 1, is quoted), when it is an epithet, in the vocative, of Pûshan. In both places the

[1] Prof. Wilson has misunderstood the latter of the two words when he translates it, "not spreading or dispersing." See his note *in loco.*

word is rendered by *annavat*, "having food." *Anushvadham* is found in R.V. i. 81, 4; ii. 3, 11; iii. 47, 1.[1] In the first of these texts Sâyaṇa explains it to mean "during the drinking of food in the shape of soma;" in the second by "at every oblation" (*prati haviḥ*); and in the third by "followed by," or "following," the oblations (*savanîya-puroḍâṣâdi-rûpeṇânnenânugatam* ...... *svadhâm anugamya varttamânam*). The words *anu svadhâm* are found separately in R.V. i. 33, 11; viii. 77, 5; and in the reverse order *svadhâm anu* in i. 6, 4, and viii. 20, 7.[2] In the first of these texts Sâyaṇa renders the words by "the waters flowed *with reference to* Indra's *food in the shape of rice*," etc. (*annaṃ vrîhy-âdi-rûpam anulakshya*); in the second (viii. 77, 5), by "*after* our *food* or *water*;" in the third (i. 6, 4), by "*with reference to the food or water* which was about to be produced;"[3] and in the fourth (viii. 20, 7), by, "with reference to food having the character of an oblation." *Svadhayâ* is found in R.V. i. 64, 4, applied to the Maruts, where it is correctly rendered by Sâyaṇa *svakîyena balena*, "by their own strength." In iv. 13, 5, too, *kayâ svadhayâ* is explained as = *kena balena*, "by what strength?" It also occurs in vii. 78, 4; ix. 71, 8; x. 27, 19; x. 88, 1; x. 129, 2. In the first of these passages the word is rendered by *annena*, "by food."[4] Surely there can be little doubt that here it means "by its own power," "spontaneously." To say, "she (Ushas) ascended her car yoked *by food*,[5] which her well-yoked horses

[1] It also occurs in ix. 72, 5; but I have no access to Sâyaṇa's Comm. on that passage.

[2] See also R.V. i. 165, 5; vii. 56, 13.

[3] Sâyaṇa here gives the following derivation of *svadhâ*, viz.: *svam lokam dadhâti pushṇâti iti svadhâ*. This word has three senses assigned to it in the Nighaṇṭus, viz. "water" (i. 12), "food" (ii. 7), and "heaven and earth" in the dual (iii. 30).

[4] The same general sense is assigned in i. 154, 4; v. 34, 1: vii. 47, 3. See also Sâyaṇa on i. 164. 38.

[5] I am not aware that in any passage the chariots or horses of the gods are said to be yoked by food, as denoted by any word which certainly bears that sense. The horses of Indra are, indeed, represented as being yoked by prayer (*brahma-yuj*) in R.V. i. 177, 2; iii. 35, 4; viii. 1, 24; viii. 2, 27; viii. 2, 17; and as being yoked by a hymn (*vacho-yuj*) in viii. 45, 39; but in these cases, generally, at least, the god is supposed to yoke his car in consequence of this invitation to come and partake of the oblation, or libation, and not after partaking of it. It is true that the word *brahman* (neuter) has sometimes the sense of "food" or "oblation" ascribed to it, and that in two of the above texts, viii. 1, 24, and viii. 2, 27, one of the optional senses assigned by Sâyaṇa to *brahma-yuj* is, "yoked by our oblation," two other senses, "yoked by the lord, Indra," and "yoked by o

bring hither," makes but an indifferent sense, whilst it would yield an appropriate poetical meaning to say that she ascended her car yoked "by its own inherent power." Compare R.V. iv. 26, 4, where the phrase *achakrayâ svadhayâ* is rendered by Sâyaṇa a "wheel-less car," the word *svadhâ* having here, he says, the sense of chariot (*atra svadhâ-ṣabdo ratha-vâchî*); and for proof he refers to R.V. x. 27, 19,[1] where we have the words *achakrayâ svadhayâ varttamânam*, etc., "I beheld the troop borne from afar, moving by a wheel-less *inherent power*," which is no doubt the proper rendering in iv. 26, 4, also. It is clear that *svadhâ* could not have the sense of chariot in vii. 78, 4, above cited, as it would be absurd to speak of the *car* (*ratha*) of Ushas being yoked by a *car* (*svadhâ*). Having no access to Sâyaṇa's comment on x. 27, 19, I am not aware how he translates it; but he probably adheres to the rendering given on iv. 26, 4, as it would make nonsense to say, "moving by wheel-less *food*."[2] As regards R.V. x. 129, 2, 5, I gather from Mr. Colebrooke's translation (Misc. Essays, i. 34), than even Sâyaṇa abandons the sense of food as appropriate in that hymn, since *svadhâ* is there rendered by "her who is sustained within him." It seems, however, better to render it in verse 2 by "through its inherent power," and in *v.* 5, by "a self-supporting principle." The sense, "by their own power" seems appropriate in x. 88, 1, though here too it is rendered by "food," Nir. vii. 25. *Svadhâbhiḥ* (*loc.* pl.) is explained in i. 95, 4, and i. 164, 30, by "sacrificial food;" in v. 60, 4. by "waters;" in vii. 104, 9, by "forces;" and in viii. 10, 4, by "praises which are the cause of strength." I come lastly to *svadhâvat*, which I find in R.V. v. 3, 2; vi. 58, 1; vii. 20, 1; vii. 37, 2; vii. 46, 1; vii. 86, 5, and elsewhere. In vi. 58, 1, and vii. 46, 1, as we have already seen, the word is rendered by Yâska, "having food;" and in

hymn," being proposed in the former case, and one alternative sense, "yoked by our hymn," being proposed in the latter. In i. 177, 2; iii. 35, 4; and viii. 17, 2, however, "yoked by our hymn" (*mantra*) is the only rendering given. *Vacho-yuj* in viii. 45, 39, is explained, "yoked by our hymn."

[1] This and some other instances show that Sâyaṇa did occasionally resort to parallel passages for the elucidation of the text under his consideration, but he did not carry the practice far enough.

[2] Compare *achakrebhiḥ* in R.V. v. 42, 10, and *nichakrayâ* in viii. 7, 29.

these passages (as well as in vii. 31, 7; vii. 88, 5), he is followed by Sâyaṇa, who, again, in i. 95, 4; v. 3, 2, translates it by "having sacrificial food." In vi. 21, 3; vii. 20, 1; vii. 37, 2; and vii. 86, 4, however, Sâyaṇa departs from Yâska, and from his own practice elsewhere, in rendering *svadhâvat* by *balavat* or *tejasvin*, "strong," or "vigorous." Prof. Roth has treated of *anushvadham*, etc., in his Illustrations of the Nirukta, pp. 40 f.; and in his Lexicon he translates the word in question by "willingly," "spontaneously," "gladly." In his new translation of the R.V., in the "Orient und Occident," Prof. Benfey renders *svadhâm anu*, *anu svadhâm*, and *anushvadham*, in i. 6, 4; i. 33, 11; and i. 81, 4, in a similar manner. This interpretation, in fact, will probably be found to suit nearly all, if not the whole, of the texts in which the phrase is found.

Aprâyu is explained in Nir. iv. 19, where R.V. i. 89, 1, is quoted, as meaning in that passage (where it is an epithet of the gods) *apramâdyantaḥ*, "not careless." Sâyaṇa, in his comment on the same text, declares it to be equivalent to *apragachhantaḥ svakîyam rakshitavyam aparityajyantaḥ*, "not departing, not forsaking him whom they have to protect." (Mahîdhara, the commentator on the Vâj. S. (where this text is repeated, xxv. 14), explains the word by *anâlasâḥ*, "not sluggish.") The word occurs again in R.V. viii. 24, 18, as an epithet of sacrifices, where Sâyaṇa interprets it to mean *either* sacrifices which are conducted by men who are "not careless" (*apramâdyat*), *or* by "careful men who perform the rite remaining together, and do not go elsewhere after they have begun it." In the first passage, at least, he departs from Sâyaṇa. Prof. Goldstücker, *s.v.*, renders the word "attentive," "assiduous," adding, "according to Yâska . . .; but Sâyaṇa gives to this word in one verse the meaning, 'not going forth, not leaving' . . . .; while in another he admits also the former meaning, which seems more congenial to the context."

Ambhriṇa is given in Nigh. iii. 3, as one of the synonyms of *mahat*, "great." It occurs in R.V. i. 133, 5, as an epithet of *piṣâchi*, "a goblin," and is interpreted by Sâyaṇa as meaning *either* "shrieking very terribly" *or* "very huge." It is clear, therefore, that Sâyaṇa did not know by any certain tradition what the sense of the word was.

Amyak.—This word is found in one of the passages which Kautsa (see above) charges with obscurity, R.V. i. 169, 3; *amyak sâ te Indra ṛshṭir asme;* and I therefore think it as well to give some account of it, although it does not afford any very strong evidence in favour of any of the propositions I have undertaken to establish. Yâska, Nir. vi. 15, explains the term by *amâkteti vâ abhyakteti vâ*, meaning apparently either "arrived near," or "arrived towards." The fact of his giving an alternative etymology shows that he did not know for certain what the real derivation was, though his mind may have been made up as to the sense. Prof. Roth (Illustrations of Nir. p. 81) considers *amyak* to be the third per. aor. of *myaksh*, which, from a comparison of other passages, he believes to have the sense of "gleaming." The words would thus mean: "Thy bolt *gleamed* upon us, o Indra." Sâyaṇa, without offering any etymology, translates the clause thus: "Thy thunderbolt *comes* (*prâpnoti*) near the clouds for us, for rain to us." As both Yâska (in the passage above cited) and Sâyaṇa in his introduction to the R.V. (p. 5 of Müller's edition) had referred to and ridiculed the objection taken against the intelligibility of this verse, they were bound in honour to make it yield some sense or other; though from the obscurity of which it was cited as an instance—perhaps a proverbial instance—even so far back as the time of the former, it seems difficult to suppose that they had any certain tradition to go upon as to its meaning. Prof. Goldstücker translates the word *amyak* (see *s.v.*) "towards, near;" and adds: "This is apparently the meaning of the word in the following Rig-veda verse, where it seems to be used with the ellipsis of 'come.'" He then, after quoting the verse before us, goes on: "Yaska, who, in a discussion in his introduction, denies that this word can be called obscure, renders it in this verse *amâkteti vâbhyakteti vâ*, 'come here,' or 'come towards;' and Sâyaṇa explains it by *prâpnoti*, without, however, giving its etymology. This formation of the word corresponds with that of other compounds ending iu *ach.*" Prof. Goldstücker holds that it would be "against all grammatical analogy" to take *amyak* for an aorist, as Roth proposes. There is no proof, however, that either Yâska or Sâyaṇa concurred with Prof. Goldstücker in holding the word for a particle in *ach.*

Alâtṛṇa occurs in two passages of the Rig-veda. One of these, iii. 30, 10, is quoted in Nir. vi. 2, where it is explained as = *alam âtardanaḥ,* "greatly-splitting, or split." If this explanatory phrase be understood in the passive sense, it will coincide with Sâyaṇa's interpretation, "that which, from being full of water, is exceedingly broken." In i. 166, 7, the word is an epithet of the Maruts, and is explained by Sâyaṇa as susceptible of three different senses, viz., as standing either—1st, for *anâtṛṇâsaḥ* = *âtardana-rahitâḥ,* "free from splitting;" or, 2nd, as *alam âtardanâḥ ṣatrûṇâm,* "great cleavers of their enemies;" or, 3rd, as *alam dâtâraḥ phalânâm,* "great bestowers of rewards." Who will say that Sâyaṇa is here either a confident, or a satisfactory, guide?

Askṛdhoyu is explained by Yâska (in Nir. vi. 3, where he quotes R.V. vi. 22, 3) as = *akṛdhv-âyuḥ,* "not short-lived;" *kṛdhu,* being = *hrasva,* "short." Sâyaṇa renders it in two passages (vi. 22, 3; vi. 67, 11) by *avichhinna,* "not cut off," which would coincide with Yâska's interpretation; but on vii. 53, 3, he takes it for *ahrasvam analpam,* "not short," "not little," which seems to differ somewhat from the former sense, inasmuch as it refers not to duration but to quantity.

Asridh does not occur in the Nirukta. It is variously interpreted by Sâyaṇa either as "free from decay," or "desiccation" (i. 3, 9; i. 13, 9), or as "free from desiccation, always remaining in the same state (the Maruts," i. 89, 3), or as "innocuous" (iv. 32, 24; iv. 45, 4; v. 46, 4).

Ahimanyu does not occur in the Nirukta. It is applied to the Maruts in R.V. i. 64, 8, where Sâyaṇa offers a choice of interpretations, making it either = *âhanana-ṣîla-manyu-yuktâḥ,* "filled with wrath disposed to smite," or = *ahîna-jnânâḥ,* "of eminent wisdom." He was, therefore, only guessing at the sense.

Ahimâya is not found in the Nirukta. It is understood by

Sâyaṇa on i. 190, 4, as an epithet of Vṛttra and his class, and translated as either = "those whose enchantments come and destroy," or "those whose enchantments come in the atmosphere." On vi. 20, 7, he understands it as = "those who have destructive enchantments;" and on vi. 52, 15, as = "those who have destructive wisdom." I am not aware how he renders it in x. 63, 4. Another epithet of the gods, *ehimâya*, which Roth thinks may be a corruption of *ahimâya*, occurs in R.V. i. 3, 9, where Sâyaṇa assigns two possible senses—1st, "having all-pervading wisdom;" and, 2nd, that of a designation of the deities, derived from their having said to Agni when he had entered into the waters, *ehi mâ yâsîḥ*, "come, do not go."

Âṣuṣukshaṇi, which occurs R.V. ii. 1, 1, and Vâj. S. xi. 27, as an epithet of Agni, is explained in Nir. vi. 1 as meaning either "one who quickly slays, or gives, by his flame" (*âṣu ṣuchâ kshaṇoti iti vâ sanoti iti vâ*), or "desiring to consume." Sâyaṇa translates the word "flaming on all sides," or "one who quickly gives pain to his enemies by consuming," etc. Mahîdhara, on Vâj. S. xi. 27, translates *âṣuṣukshaṇi* as either = "quickly drying the wet ground," or as = "quickly destroying the darkness with his flame, or giving, distributing, by his flame." Roth (Illustrations of Nirukta, p. 72) compares *ṣuṣukvani* in R.V. viii. 23, 5, where Sâyaṇa renders "glowing."

Âsâ occurs frequently in the Rig-veda, and is diversely explained by Sâyaṇa. In his comments on ii. 1, 14; iv. 5, 10; vi. 3, 4; vi. 32, 1, he renders it by *âsyena*, "with the mouth;" on v. 17, 2, by *âsyena vâchâ*, "with the mouth, by speech;" on v. 17, 5; v. 23, 1, by *âsyena stotreṇa*, "with the mouth, with a hymn;" on i. 76, 4; vi. 16, 9, by *âsyena âsya-sthânîyayâ* (or *âsya-bhûtayâ*) *jvâlayâ*, "with the mouth, with the flame in the mouth;" on vii. 16, 9, as an epithet of *jihvayâ*, "the tongue," by *âsya-sthânîyayâ*, "situated in the mouth;" on i. 129, 5, by "near, in the place of sacrifice;" and on i. 168, 2, by "near." Similarly, he varies in the sense of *âsayâ*, making it stand in one place (i. 20, 1) for "with the mouth," and in another (i. 127, 8) for "near."

In the Nighaṇṭus, ii. 16, the word *âsât* is found as one of the synonyms of "near."

Ishmin is variously interpreted by Sâyaṇa in different places, viz., on i. 87, 6, and vii. 56, 11, as "going, moving;" on v. 52, 16; v. 87, 5, as "going," or "possessing food." Yâska gives the three derivations of *îshaṇinaḥ*, *eshaṇinaḥ*, and *arshaṇinaḥ* (Nir. iv. 16).

Îvat.—This word occurs in R.V. iv. 4, 6; iv. 15, 5; iv. 43, 3; v. 49, 5; vi. 73, 2; vii. 23, 1; vii. 56, 18; viii. 46, 21. In all these passages, without exception, Sâyaṇa renders it either simply by "going," "moving," or by some modification of that sense, as "coming," "approaching," "coming with prosperity," "occupied," "moving creatures." And yet there seems no reason to doubt that the word signifies "so much," "so great," as it is explained by Roth, *s.v.*, as being an old Vedic form for *iyat*, just as *kîvat* is for *kiyat*, as is (in the latter case) recognised both by Yâska (Nir. vi. 3) and by Sâyaṇa on R.V. iii. 30, 17, the only passage where it occurs. From this it appears that just as in ordinary Sanskrit *îdṛk* and *kîdṛk* are formed in the same way as *etâdṛk*, *tâdṛk*, *yâdṛk*, so, too, in ancient times the series of *etâvat*, *tâvat*, *yâvat*, was completed by *îvat* and *kîvat*, though at a subsequent period the two latter forms became obsolete, whilst *iyat* and *kiyat*, which are also found in the R.V., were regarded as alone correct. Their sense of "so much," "so great," etc. etc., appears, as far as I can judge, to suit all the passages of the R.V. where the word *îvat* occurs.

Urugâya (generally an epithet of Vishṇu) is interpreted by Yâska (Nir. ii. 7) in his comment on R.V. i. 154, 6, as = *mahâgati*, "making large strides." Sâyaṇa, however, wavers in his explanation, making it either "hymned by many" (on i. 154, 3; ii. 1, 3); "wide-going," or "much-praised" (on iii. 6, 4); "hymned by many," or "of great renown" (on iv. 3, 7); "great goers" (of the Aṣvins, iv. 14, 1); "celebrated by many" (on vii. 100, 1); "to be hymned by many," or "moving in many places," or "of great renown," or "one who, by his power, makes all his enemies howl" (on viii. 29, 7); "hymned by the great" (on i. 154, 1); "to be hymned by many great persons" (i. 154, 6). See also i. 155, 4; vi. 28, 4; vi. 65, 6; vii. 35, 15; x. 109, 7, where Prof. Roth considers the word to be a substantive. Looking to R.V. i. 22, 16 ff., about the striding of Vishṇu, there can be little doubt that the adjective *urugâya* means "wide-striding."

Ṛdûdara occurs in R.V. viii. 48, 10, as an epithet of Soma, and is interpreted by Yâska (vi. 4) in his explanation of part of that verse as = *mṛdûdara*, and as meaning "soft-bellied," or "soft in (men's) bellies." Sâyaṇa (on the same verse) renders it, "not hurting the belly" (*udarâbâdhakena*). On ii. 33, 5, where the word is applied to Rudra, he adopts the first of Yâska's two meanings; whilst on iii. 54, 10, where it is applied to the Âdityas, he repeats both of his predecessor's interpretations, modifying the second so as to signify, "those in whose bellies Soma is soft."[1]

Ṛjîshin, according to Yâska (v. 12, where he explains R.V. x. 89, 5), means Soma, but is also an epithet of Indra. "That which remains of soma when it is being purified is *ṛjîsha*, or rejected; therefore *ṛjîshin* is soma. There is also a text referring to Indra as *ṛjîshî vajrî*." Mahîdhara, on Vâj. S. xix. 72, says that *ṛjîsha* is the squeezed and juiceless refuse of the soma-plant. Sâyaṇa generally interprets the word *ṛjîshin* as an epithet of Indra by, "he who has the soma after it has been pressed and has lost its juice or taste" (on iii. 32, 1; iii. 36, 10; iv. 16, 1, 5; vi. 20, 2). On i. 64, 12, and i. 87, 1, where *ṛjîshin* is an epithet of the Maruts, he explains that at the third libation when those deities are worshipped this *ṛjîsha* is offered, and hence they are said to have it. On v. 40, 4 (where the word is applied to Indra) he says that after the soma has been offered at the first and second libations, and has become juiceless, that which is offered at the third libation is called *ṛjîsha* = *soma*. On iii. 46, 3, he makes *ṛjîshin* simply equivalent to *somavân*, "having soma." In two places, however, where the word is applied to the Maruts, Sâyaṇa gives alternative interpretations, viz., on ii.

[1] The Sanskrit scholar may also examine Yâska's desperate attempt (vi. 33) to explain the two words *ṛdûpâ* and *ṛdûvṛdh*, which occur in R.V. viii. 66, 11. Sâyaṇa merely repeats Yâska; but his text of the passage differs somewhat from Roth's.

34, 1, he says it means either "having water," or "having tasteless soma;" and on i. 87, 1, "either having such soma, or, being providers(?) of moisture" (*prârjayitâro rasânâm*). In i. 32, 6, where the word *ṛjîsha* (not *-shin*) is applied to Indra, Sâyaṇa makes it=*ṣatrûṇâm apârjakam*, "repeller of enemies." It thus appears that he wavers in his interpretation. The sense of "drinker of tasteless or spiritless soma" is not a very probable one. Indra is generally represented as greatly exhilarated by the beverage he quaffs, and it seems a poor compliment to him to call him the drinker of a vapid draught. Besides, in one of the texts of which *ṛjîshin* is the first word, *soma-pâvan*, a term which indubitably means soma-drinker, is found at the end of the same line, and it is unlikely that two epithets so closely resembling each other as "soma-drinker" and "spiritless-soma-drinker" should occur so near. In his glossary to the Sâma-veda, and in his translation of S.V. i. 248 and ii. 789, Prof. Benfey renders the word by "victorious;" and it appears from his note on the last of these two texts that the commentator there gives a choice of interpretations. Prof. Roth *s.v.* translates it by "forward-rushing;" and Benfey, in his translation of R.V. i. 87, 1, renders it similarly by "gradaus schreitenden" (Orient und Occident, ii. 249).

Evayâvan, which is not found in the Nirukta, is diversely interpreted by Sâyaṇa as="moving with horses" (applied by him to the Maruts, i. 90, 5); as="going to the hymn or sacrifice to which they should go" (ii. 34, 11, spoken of the same); as="moving with horses, or with the waters of the atmosphere,—coming with showers for the pleasure of others also" (vi. 48, 12, *evayâvart*, spoken of the cow); or as="bringing to his worshippers the objects which they desire to obtain" (on vii. 100, 2, spoken of Vishṇu).

Kâṇukâ is one of the terms objected to by Kautsa as obscure (see above). It occurs only once, in R.V. viii. 66, 4; and Yâska does his utmost to explain it in Nir. v. 11. The whole verse runs thus: "Indra drank at one draught thirty lakes (or cups) of soma. . . . . ," the word *kâṇukâ* being the last of the verse. Yâska takes it either for a neuter plural, agreeing with *saràṃsi* (cups) and meaning "desired" (*kântakâni*), or "entirely full" (*krântakâni*), or "properly formed" (*kṛtakâni*), or for an epithet of Indra, signifying "fond or beloved of soma" (*somasya kântaḥ*), or "overcome by love of soma" (*kaṇe ghâta iti vâ kaṇe hataḥ kântihataḥ*). "The ritualists" (*yâjnikâḥ*), (Yâska proceeds), "say that the thirty bowls which are destined for one deity at the mid-day libations, and are drunk off at once, are denoted in this verse by the word *saràṃsi*, whilst the etymologists (*nairuktâḥ*), consider that they stand for the thirty nights and days constituting respectively the first and second halves of the month. In the second half the rays drink up the collected waters of the moon." According to the latter interpretation, Indra is (as Sâyaṇa remarks) the deity personifying time (*kâlâbhimânî*). In his explanation Sâyaṇa merely abridges Yâska's.

Kârudhayaḥ is in three places (vi. 21, 8 : vi. 24, 2 ; vi. 44, 12) explained by Sâyaṇa as "upholder of poets or worshippers" (*kârûṇâṃ dhârakaḥ*, or *dhârayitâ*.) In another passage (iii. 32, 10) he gives a different sense, "maker of works" (*karmaṇâṃ vidhâtâ*). This latter sense would be appropriate enough here if it exists in the component elements of the word.

Kiyedhâḥ is explained by Yâska (vi. 20, where he quotes R.V. i. 61, 12), in two ways, as = either to *kiyaddhâḥ* "holding how much?" or to *kramamâṇa-dhâḥ*, "holding those who advance." Sâyaṇa, on i. 61, 6, renders it by *balavân*, "strong," and declares the two interpretations of the Nirukta to mean (1) "one who has strength of which no one knows the extent," and (2) "one who stops the advancing might of others. On verse 12 of the same hymn, he repeats the same explanations. It appears from Roth's Illustrations, *in loco*, that Durga, the commentator on the Nirukta, refers the epithet to Vṛttra, whilst others referred it to Indra. And Roth remarks, that by his double interpretation, "holding how much (water or power)?" and "holding the advancing (waters or hostile powers)," Yâska has left the application to one or other of these personages open.

Kuchara is explained by Yâska i. 20 (where R.V. i. 154, 2, is quoted), as meaning (if applied to a wild beast) "doing an evil deed," or if taken for a designation of the god (Vishṇu), as signifying "whither does he not go?" Sâyaṇa, on the same passage, gives it the sense either of "door of evil deeds, such as killing," or "going to inaccessible places," or, if understood of the gods, as meaning either "doing evil deeds, such as the slaughter of enemies," or "one who ranges in all places throughout the three worlds." (*Kushu, sarvâsu bhûmishu, lokatraye, sanchârî.*) We have thus between Yâska and Sâyaṇa three derivations, according as we conceive the word to be compounded of *ku*, "bad," *ku*, "earth," or *kva*, "where," prefixed to *chara*, "going," or "acting." Such a play upon words in a double sense, though common enough in the modern rhetorical poetry of the Hindus, is scarcely to be looked for in the ancient hymns of the Veda.

Kuṇâru is explained by Yâska (Nir. vi. 1, where he quotes R. V. iii. 30, 8) as meaning a "cloud" (*parikvaṇanam megham*). Sâyaṇa (on the same passage) gives two interpretations of the words *sahadânuṃ kshiyantaṃ saṃ piṇak kuṇârum*, viz., either (1) "crush the destroying (*kshiyantaṃ*) *kuṇâru* = a certain yelling Asura, associated with Dânu, Vṛttra's mother, or with the Dânavas," or (2) "Crush the thundering (*kuṇâru*) Vṛttra, having the gift of bestowing water (*sahadânum*), dwelling (*kshiyantam*) in the sky." Thus there are no less than three words in this single line (viz., *sahâdanum, kshiyantam,* and *kuṇârum*), of which Sâyaṇa offers alternative explanations.

Kshayadvîra does not occur in the Nirukta. It is variously explained by Sâyaṇa as "very strong, he in whom all heroes are destroyed" (on i. 106, 4); or, "he in whom heroes perish, or whose sons, the Maruts, rule" (on i. 114, 1, 2); or "he who has heroes, sons and servants, dwelling with him" (on i. 125, 3); or "possessed of heroes, sons and others, dwelling or moving" (*nivasadbhir itvarair vâ*, on R.V. viii. 19, 10). It will be seen, that as regards the root *kshi*, which forms the first member of this compound, Sâyaṇa wavers between the three senses of "perishing," "ruling," and "dwelling."

Girikshit, an epithet of Vishṇu (in i. 154, 3), is translated by Sâyaṇa as "residing in speech" (*giri* locative of *gir*), or "in a region high as a mountain." In this passage, however, it has, probably, one single sense.

Jâtûbharman is not in the Nirukta. Sâyaṇa explains it as meaning either "having the lightning for a weapon," or "supporter of creatures."

Jârayâyi is another of the words objected to by Kautsa as obscure. (See above.) It occurs only once in the R.V., vi. 12, 4, which is quoted by Yâska in vi. 15, where he explains it by *ajâyi*, to which his commentator Durga gives the meaning "is, or was, born." (See Roth's Illustrations, etc , p. 82.) Sâyaṇa, on the contrary, renders it by *stûyate* "is praised."

Jîradânu is not found in the Nirukta, though *jîra* is given in the Nighaṇṭus, ii. 15, as one of the synonymes of *kshipra*, "quick." In one passage (i. 165, 15) it is rendered by Sâyaṇa *jayu-ṣîla-dânam*, "having victorious gifts;" but in all the following texts he takes it for, "whose gifts are quick" (ii. 34, 4; v. 53, 5; v. 54, 9; v. 62, 3; v. 83, 1; vii. 64, 2; viii. 51, 3).

Joshavâka is found in R.V. vi. 59, 4, and is explained by Yâska (v. 21, 22, where he quotes this passage) as "that of which the name is unknown, that which is to be pondered (?)" *avijnâta-nâmadheyaṃ joshayitavyaṃ bhavati*). He renders the whole verse thus: "Ye, o Indra and Agni, eat the offering of the man who praises you when the soma libations are poured out. Ye do not eat (that) of the prater (?) who speaks *joshavâka*." Sâyaṇa renders: "Ye, o Indra and Agni, do not eat the (offering) of the man who, when the soma-libations are poured out, praises you badly, who, in the midst of them, speaks unpleasing words when he ought to speak pleasing ones." It is to be observed, however—and I perceive that Wilson also, in his note on the passage, has adverted to the fact—that in the quotation made from Yâska (v. 22) in Müller's edition of the R.V., the reading of the passage is different from what it is in Professor Roth's edition, as in Roth's text the first clause has no negative particle (*na*), whilst the negative particle is found there in Müller's. The meaning of that clause of the Nirukta is thus reversed. The sense given by Roth's reading appears to me to be the most conformable to the apparent meaning of Yâska, as two kinds of worshippers evidently appear to be contemplated in his explanation, one of whom the two gods approve and whose oblation they eat, and another whose oblation they do not eat. Sâyaṇa, in conformity with the reading of Yâska given by Müller, makes both clauses of the verse relate to one kind of worshipper, *i.e.*, to one whose offering the two gods disapprove. There would thus appear to be a difference between Yâska and Sâyaṇa as to the sense of the verse of the R.V. which they are expounding. What is its real sense, it is not necessary for me to decide. Roth considers that the future participle *joshayitavyam*, employed by Yâska, means "requiring consideration." Wilson renders the clause of which it forms a part, "that being of unknown name is to be propitiated." (Compare Roth's Lexicon, *s.v.*, and his remarks in his Illustr. of Nir. p. 68.)

Daksha-pitaraḥ is an epithet of the gods which is not found in the Nirukta. It occurs in three passages of the R.V. On the first (vi. 50, 2) Sâyaṇa takes the word for "those who have Daksha for their forefather," and refers to two other texts (R.V. x. 15, 3, and x. 72, 5)), the one to prove that the word *pitṛ* may stand for "forefather," and the second to show that the gods are elsewhere declared to have Daksha for their ancestor. On the second passage (vii. 66, 2) Sâyaṇa translates the word by "preservers, or lords, *i.e.* givers, of strength;" and on the third (viii. 52, 10) by "preservers, lords, of food." The word also occurs in the Taittirîya Sanhitâ, i. 2, 3, 1, where the commentator explains it much as Sâyaṇa on vi. 50, 2, does; and in Vâj. S. xiv. 3, where it is explained by "preserver of vigour."

Danaḥ is a word occurring in R.V. i. 174, 2, in regard to which Yâska (vi. 31) and Sâyaṇa contradict each other; the former taking it for an adjective meaning "liberally-minded" (*dâna-manasaḥ*), whilst the latter makes it a verb in the second person singular imperfect, meaning either "thou didst subdue," or "thou didst cause to cry."

Dasrâ, a frequent dual epithet of the Aṣvins, and sometimes of other gods (Indra and Vishṇu, vi. 69, 7), is explained by Yâska (vi. 26, where he quotes R.V. i. 117, 21), as=*darṣanîyau,* "to be seen, sightly." Sâyaṇa sometimes understands it in that sense (as on i. 47, 6; i. 117, 5, 20, 21; i. 118, 3; i. 120, 4; vi. 69, 7; viii. 22, 17); sometimes as "destroyers of enemies" (on i. 92, 16; i. 139, 3; i. 158, 1; i. 180, 5; i. 182, 2; i. 183, 4; iii. 58, 3; iv. 43, 4; v. 75, 2); once, at least, as either "destroyers of enemies," or "from their being the physicians of the gods, destroyers of diseases" (on i. 3, 3); sometimes as either "to be seen," or as "destroyers of enemies" (on viii. 5, 2; viii. 8, 1; viii. 26, 6; viii. 75, 1); sometimes as gods "having the name of Dasrâ," or as "to be seen" (on i. 116, 10). See my article on the Aṣvins, above, p. 5, note. It appears from Roth's Illustrations of Nirukta, p. 92, that Durga, the commentator on the Nirukta, explains Dasrâ by "destroyers of enemies," or "causers of works, agriculture," etc.

Divishṭi is explained by Yâska (vi. 22, where he quotes R.V. viii. 4, 19), as, in the loc. pl.=*divaḥ eshaṇeshu,* "longings after the sky." Sâyaṇa, on the same passage, makes it mean "sacrificial rites which are the causes of obtaining heaven." Similarly, on iv. 9, 2, he makes it = *yâgeshu,* "sacrifices." On iv. 46, 1, he takes it for "sacrifices which confer heaven," or "our longings after heaven being the causes."[1] And, again, on iv. 47, 1, he interprets it *divo dyulokasya eshaṇeshu satsu,* "there being longings after the sky;" on i. 139, 4, he translates, "longings after heaven, or longings, or goings, of sacrifice which enlightens, being causes;" on i. 86, 4, he renders it by "sacrificial days;" on viii. 65, 9, by "the arrivals of our days, or longings for heaven, being causes;" on vii. 74, 1, by "people who desire heaven, priests;" and on i. 141, 6, "longings after days being the cause."

Dvibarhas means, according to Yâska (vi. 17, where he quotes R.V. vi. 19, 1), "lord (*parivṛdhaḥ*) in both regions, the middle and the upper" (*i.e.* atmosphere and sky). Sâyaṇa,

[1] Sâyaṇa's note on this verse (iv. 46, 1) affords another instance of his referring to a parallel text (R.V. vii. 92, 1) to prove that the first draught of soma was offered to Vâyu.

on the same passage, and also on iv. 5, 3; vii. 24, 2; viii. 15, 2, follows Yâska. On i. 71, 6, he has, "grown (*vṛṃhito varddhitaḥ*) in the middle and upper regions." On i. 114, 10, he makes it, "lord in the two regions, the earth and the sky, or in the two paths, the southern and the northern, or lord of knowledge and of works." On i. 176, 5, he renders it, *stotra-havî-rûpa-dvividha-parivṛḍha-karmavataḥ-yajamânasya*, "of the worshipper who is eminent in both kinds of worship, *i.e.* hymns and oblations."

Nichumpuṇa is explained by Yâska (v. 17, 18, where he quotes R.V. viii. 82, 22), as a designation of soma, "that which pleases by being swallowed" (*nichânta-pṛṇo nichamanena prîṇâti*). The ocean, too, he says, is called *nichumpuṇa*; as is also the *avabhṛtha* (or cleansing of vessels and worshippers after a sacrifice), as that "in which they sound lowly, or place lowly" (*nîchair asmin kvaṇanti nîchair dadhati iti vâ*). Sâyaṇa explains in conformity with Yâska. The word also occurs in the Vâjasaneyi Sanhitâ, iii. 48, and viii. 27, on the former of which passages Mahîdhara explains it as meaning either "slow-going" (*nitarâṃ chopati mandaṃ gachhati nichumpuṇaḥ*), or "that in which they sound lowly, perform the rite with a low voice." On viii. 27, he mentions only the first of these two explanations. The sense of the word is thus left doubtful.

Naichâṣâkha and *pramaganda* are two words occurring in R.V. iii. 53, 14, a text which is quoted and explained in Nir. vi. 32. Yâska there gives various senses to *pramaganda*. He first says *maganda* is "a usurer." The descendant of such a person is *pramaganda*, "a person sprung from a very usurious family." Or, secondly, the word is $=$*pramadakaḥ*, "one who desires that there should be no future state." Or, thirdly, it it is $=$*paṇḍ.ikaḥ*, a "catamite," or "eunuch." He derives *naichâṣâkha* from *nîchâṣâkha*, apparently "of a low stock." Sâyaṇa understands it of the property of degraded people. He adopts the first of the three senses of *pramaganda* proposed by Yâska. It appears from an objection made to the eternity of the Veda which Sâyaṇa quotes in his Introduction, p. 7, and answers in p. 10 (as cited in Sanskrit Texts, iii. 62), that

Pramaganda was considered by the objectors to be the name of a king, and *Naichâṣâkha* that of a town.

Nema is given in Nir. iii. 20 as = *arddha*, "half," in which sense it is taken by Sâyaṇa on R.V. v. 61, 8. In other places (i. 54, 8; iv. 24, 4, 5; vi. 16, 18), he translates it by "these," "some," "others." But in viii. 89, 3, he holds it to be the proper name of a descendant of Bhrigu. In this he appears to be wrong. Compare R.V. ii. 12, 5.

Nishshidh, nishshidhvan, puru-nishshidh, puru-nishshidhvan. These words are not found in the Nighaṇṭus or Nirukta. The first of them, which occurs in the R.V. in different numbers and cases, is variously interpreted by Sâyaṇa in different places; as = "constantly discharging rain-clouds" (on R.V. i. 169, 2); or "commands, ordinances" (*anuṣâsanâni*, iii. 51, 5);[1] or "destructive light" (*hiṃsikâṃ dîptim*, iii. 55, 8); "hinderers, enemies" (iv. 24, 1), or "hindrances to enemies," or "cords to restrain enemies" (vi. 44, 11). *Nishshidhvarîḥ* (the feminine form of *nishshidhvan*) occurs in iii. 55, 22, where Sâyaṇa makes it = *nitarâṃ tvat-kartṛka-siddhimatyaḥ, i.e.*, "having eminently perfections created by thee" (Indra). *Puru-nishshidh* is found in i. 10, 5[2] as an epithet of Indra, and is there translated by Sâyaṇa as = "hinderer of many enemies; and *puru-nishshidhvan*, in iv. 38, 2, as a designation of Dadhikrâ, where it is understood by him in the same sense. It is, therefore, quite impossible to suppose that the commentator could have had any certain tradition of the sense of these words. Prof. Wilson, who translates *pûrvîr asya nishshidho martyeshu* in iii. 51, 5, by "many are his [Indra's] prohibitions (against evil enjoined) to men," has a note on this verse, in which he remarks that "a similar phrase in a former passage [i. 10, 5] *purunishshidhe* has been rendered 'repeller of many foes:' there is no material incompatibility, the latter being a compound epithet, and the substantive in both cases being derived from *shidh*, to succeed, to go, with the preposi-

[1] We have, in his comment on this verse, a further instance of Sâyaṇa quoting another passage for illustration, as he here cites i. 10, 5 as referring to Indra's function of command. See further on.

[2] This verse is repeated in Sâma-veda i. 363, where Benfey renders it "vielgebietend," "many ruling."

tion *nir*, out, *ex*, to exclude, to prohibit." Prof. Wilson, however, while taking notice of this one passage to which Sâyaṇa himself had drawn his attention, has not adverted to the other texts which I have adduced: and when words identical in tenor with those in iii. 51, 5, are repeated in vi. 44, 11, viz., *pûrvîsh ṭe Indra nishshidho janeshu*, he translates them differently, thus: "many are the hindrances (opposed) to thee amongst men." This does not, however, correctly reproduce Sâyaṇa's meaning.

Paritakmyâ is translated "night" in Nir. xi. 25, where R.V. x. 108, 1 is explained. This sense is adopted by Prof. Müller in translating the verse. (Lectures on Language, second series, p. 464, and note.) Prof. Aufrecht, on the other hand, renders the word by "necessity." (Journal of Ger. Or. Society, vol. xiii., pp. 496 and 498.) Prof. Roth, who in his Illustr. of the Nir. had taken the same view, assigns in his Lexicon, *s.v.*, another signification, that of "wandering," as the proper one for this passage. For most other texts of the R.V. he adopts the sense of "night," "darkness." In two passages he gives it the sense of "causing anxiety," "dangerous." Sâyaṇa renders the word by "night" in i. 116, 15; iv. 43, 3; vi. 24, 9; by "dark," apparently, in v. 30, 13; by "night," or "battle," or "sacrifice," in vii. 69, 4; by "surrounding," (*paritakane nimittabhûte sati*) or "night" in iv. 41, 6; by "battle" in v. 31, 11; by "to be gone round, or surrounded," as an epithet of *dhane*, wealth, in i. 31, 6; and by "surrounding," as an epithet of *râtrî*, "night," which goes before, in v. 30, 14. It thus appears that in some places he is uncertain about the sense.

Paryabhûshat in R.V. ii. 12, 1, is explained by Yâska (x. 10) as = *paryabhavat paryagṛhṇât paryarakshad atyakrâmad iti vâ*, *i e.*, "overcame, or comprehended, or protected, or surpassed." He could not, therefore, it would appear, have been very sure of its meaning. Sâyaṇa renders simply *rakshakatvena paryagrahît*, "surrounded as a protector." The same word is found in the imperative (*pari bhûsha*) in R.V. i. 15, 4, where Sâyaṇa renders it, "adorn," and Benfey, "encircle;" and in i. 31, 2, where Sâyaṇa, followed by Benfey, translates the clause, *devâ-*

nâṃ pari bhûshasi vratam, "thou adornest the ceremonial (*karma*) of the gods." The same root, preceded by the particle *vi,* occurs in i. 112, 4, *vi bhûshati,* where Sâyaṇa offers two explanations, "is diffused," or "eminently adorns," and in vi. 15, 9, *vi bhûshan,* where he renders, "adorning." The word *âbhûsha,* in R.V. vii. 92, 1 (=Vâj. S. vii. 7) is understood by both commentators, Sâyaṇa and Mahîdhara, in the sense of "come."

Pânta is explained in Nir. vii. 25 (where R.V. x. 88, 1 is quoted) as = *pânîya,* "to be drunk." It occurs also in R.V. i. 122, 1, where Sâyaṇa renders it by "preserving, or to be drunk, sacrifice, or instrument of sacrifice." On i. 55, 1, also, he gives it the sense of either "protecting, or to be drunk."

Purukshu is not found in the Nirukta; but *kshu* is given in the Nighaṇṭus, ii. 7, as a synomyme of *anna,* "food." Sâyaṇa interprets it variously, for the most part as = *bahvanna,* "having much food" (on i. 68, 5; iii. 25, 2; iii. 54, 21; iv. 34, 10; vi. 19, 5); also as = "greatly renowned" (ii. 40, 4); as having one or other of the two preceding senses (iv. 29, 5; vi. 68, 6); and, again, as "having much food, or many cattle" (vi. 22, 3). The commentator on the Vaj. S., xxvii. 20, renders it "that which dwells in many" (*bahushu kshiyati nivasati*).

Pṛthupâjas does not occur in the Nirukta; but *pâjas* is given in the Nighaṇṭus, ii. 9, as one of the synonymes for *bala,* "strength." In Nir. vi. 12, it is said to derive its name from preserving. *Pṛthupâjas* is variously rendered by Sâyaṇa as "having great strength" (iii. 27, 5; iv. 46, 5); as "having great vigour (or lustre," *tejas,* iii. 5, 1; iii. 27, 5); as "having great strength or much food" (iii. 3, 1; viii. 5, 2); as "having great vigour (or lustre) or great velocity" (iii. 2, 11).

Pṛthushṭuka occurs as an epithet of Sinîvâlî in R.V. ii. 32, 6. This passage is quoted in Nir. xi. 32, and the word is there explained as either "broad-loined," or "having broadly plaited (or a broad mass of) hair" (*pṛthukeṣa-stuke*), or *pṛthu-stuke.* Sâyaṇa renders by *pṛthu-jaghane pṛthu-saṃhate vâ,* "having broad loins," or "broadly built" (?) The passage is repeated in Vaj. S. xxxiv. 10, where Mahîdhara makes the word = *he pṛthukeṣa-bhâre mahâstute vâ pṛthukâme vâ* "having a large mass of hair, or greatly praised, or having large desires." On the sense of the word *stukâ*, compare Weber, Ind. Stud., v. 233 and 237.

Pvadivaḥ is met with in the Nighaṇṭus, iii. 27, as one of the synonymes of *purâṇa*, "old." The same sense is assigned to it in the Nirukta, viii. 19, as well as in iv. 8, where it is rendered by *pûrveshu api ahassu* "even in former days." Sâyaṇa, in his note on the passage here illustrated by Yâska (R.V. iii. 47, 1), adheres to the interpretation of the latter. He also retains the sense "old" in i. 53, 2; ii. 3, 1; iii. 36, 2; iv. 6, 4; iv. 7, 8; v. 8, 7; vi. 5, 3; vi. 23, 5; but in iii. 38, 5 and iv. 34, 3 he assigns to the word the meaning of "extremely shining" (*prakarsheṇa dyotamâna*).

Bakura is found in R.V. i. 117, 21, a passage quoted by Yâska (vi. 25, 26), where (after saying that *bakura* is = *bhâskaro bhayankaro bhâsamâno dravati iti vâ*, "illuminator, terrible, or that which runs shining") he assigns to the word the sense of "light or water" (*jyotishâ udakena vâ*. Sâyaṇa gives it the meaning of the "shining lightning." Prof. Roth thinks it denotes a wind instrument. Whether he is right or not, it is clear that Yâska had no certain knowledge of its sense.

Bîriṭa, as we are told in Nir. v. 27, means, according to Taiṭîki, the "atmosphere," the first syllable being from *vî*, "to go," and the second being from *ir*, "to go," and the whole denoting that wherein the birds or the clouds move. Yâska then quotes the only passage in which it occurs, R.V. vii. 39, 2 (=Vâj. S. xxxiii. 44), giving it first the sense of atmosphere, and next suggesting the sense of "assemblage of men." Sâyaṇa repeats the two interpretations of Yâska. Mahîdhara adopts the second, but quotes Yâska.

Madachyut does not occur in the Nirukta. It is generally understood by Sâyaṇa as "humbler of the pride of enemies" (on R.V. i. 51, 2; i. 81. 3; viii. 1, 21; viii. 85, 5), or, "humblers of enemies," viii. 22, 16. But on i. 85, 7, he takes it for "that which sheds forth joy, the sacrifice."

Mṛdhravâch is explained by Yâska (vi. 31, where he quotes R.V. i. 174, 2) as = *mṛdu-vâchaḥ* "softly-speaking." This translation is quoted by Sâyaṇa at the end of his note on the passage without remark. His own rendering is different, as he either, according to the interpretation of the Aitihasikas (legendary writers), makes the word = *marshaṇa-vachanâḥ*, "uttering angry words," or, according to that of the Nairuktas, takes it as = *marshaṇa-dhvani-yuktâḥ*, "having a threatening sound." On v. 29, 10; v. 32, 8; and vii. 6, 3, he understands the term to stand for "with organs of speech destroyed," or "with speech destroyed;" and on vii. 18, 13, he assigns a sense similar to that given on i. 174, 2, viz., *bâdhavâcham*, "injuriously speaking." The meanings he assigns are thus mutually inconsistent, as well as at variance with that proposed by Yâska.

Amṛdhra occurs frequently in the R.V., as in v. 37, 1; v. 43, 2, 13; vi. 19, 7; vi. 22, 10; vi. 75, 9; vii. 67, 5, in all which places it is rendered by Sâyaṇa *ahiṃsita*, or *hiṃsâ-rahita*, "uninjured," or *hiṃsitum aṣakya*, "uninjurable." On iii. 58, 8, he translates "not despised by any one." On i. 37, 11, besides "uninjurable," he proposes an alternative sense, "not wetting," which Prof. Goldstücker regards as not very probable (see *s.v.*). On viii. 69, 2 (where, however, Müller puts the texts in brackets), he renders it in an active sense, *ahinsaka*, "not injuring." On Vaj. S. xxix. 46, Mahîdhara renders the word "hard-limbed, or giving stern commands."

Mehanâ (an undeclined word) is found in Nir. iv. 4 (where R.V. v. 39, 1 is quoted), and is explained as either = *maṃhanîyaṃ*[1] *dhanam*, "to be given, wealth," or *me iha na* "(that which) I have not here."[2] Sâyaṇa, following Yâska's first interpretation, understands *mehanâ* as = *maṃhanîya*, on v. 38, 3 and v. 39, 1. On viii. 4, 21, repeating both Yâska's explanations, he makes it either *maṃhanîyâṃ praṣasyâm*, "laudable,

[1] The verb *maṃh* is found in Nigh. iii. 20, as signifying "to give."

[2] See on this word Roth's Illust. of Nir. p. 39, where other passages in which it occurs are given. Roth mentions that Durga, the commentator on the Nirukta, says that, in the R.V., *mehanâ* is one word, whilst in the Sâmaveda it is considered to be made up of three. On the sense of the term see also Benfey's Gloss. to S.V., p. 151.

excellent," agreeing with both *gâm* (fem.) "cow," and *aṣra* (masc.) "horse," or, *me iha na*; and the latter words he explains thus: "In this king (*iha*) there was not (*na*) to me (*me*) that gift of excellent wealth." On viii. 52, 12 (=V.S. 33, 50), he takes the word as = *udaka-sechana-yuktâḥ*, or *sechanena yuktâḥ*, "shedding water." Mahîdhara, on the same verse, explains, "shedders of wealth," etc., *dhanâdi-sektâraḥ*. In iii. 49, 3, the word *mehanâvân* is met with, which Sâyaṇa explains thus: *mihyate sichyate dîyate arthibhyaḥ iti mehanaṃ dhanaṃ tadvân*, "*mehana* is wealth, that which is shed forth, given, to suppliants; he who has it is *mehanâvat*."

Reṇukakâṭa is not mentioned in the Nirukta. It is found as an epithet of *arvan*, "horse," in R.V. vi. 28, 4, where Sâyaṇa takes it for "stirring up dust," spoken of a horse come for battle. The word is also found connected with *arvan* in Vâj. S. xxviii. 13, where it is differently understood by Mahîdhara as follows: *kâṭaḥ kûpaḥ, kutsitaḥ kâṭah kakâṭah, reṇubhiḥ kṛtvâ kakâṭaḥ reṇukakâṭaḥ*, "*kâṭa* is a well; *kakâṭa* is a bad well; a bad well with dust is a *reṇukakâṭa*." Such a well, into which calves and youths fall, is to be removed. Wells, etc., which obstruct sacrifices and offspring are to be removed from the road. Such is this scholiast's explanation. It will be seen that the two Commentators are far from agreeing, and the word is so constructed that there is no reason to suppose it has both senses.

Vavakshitha and *vivakshase* are given in Nigh. iii. 3, among the synonymes of *mahat*, "great;" and in Nir. iii. 13, are said to be derived from the root *vach*, "to speak," or from *vah*, "to carry." Sâyaṇa seems (except in one case, vii. 100, 6), to regard the different forms of this word as coming from *vah*, "to bring," and interprets as follows: *vavakshuḥ*, "they wish to bring" (R.V. i. 64, 3); *ati vavakshitha*, "thou exceedingly wishest to carry, art a supporter of" (i. 81, 5); ditto, "thou exceedingly wishest to carry" (i. 102, 8; iii. 9, 3); *vavakshitha*, "thou wishest to carry all" (ii. 22, 3); *vavakshe* = *uvâha*, "he carried" (iv. 16, 5); *vavakshatuḥ* = *avahatâm*, "they two carried" (viii. 12, 25–27); *anuvavakshitha* =

anuvodhum ichha, "desire to carry" (viii. 77, 5). *Pravavakshe*, in vii. 100, 6, is rendered both by Yâska (v. 8) and by Sâyaṇa in loco, as=*prabrûshe*, "thou sayest." Setting aside the last passage, it appears to me that in most of the rest which I have quoted the sense of "carrying" is inappropriate. In i. 64, 3, Sâyaṇa has to supply the words, "what is desired by their worshippers," in order to make the word "bring" yield a tolerable sense; whilst, if we take the verb to signify "waxed, grew," the meaning will be "the Rudras waxed like mountains." So, too, in i. 81, 5, and i. 102, 8, it makes a better sense to say of Indra, "thou hast waxed greater than the whole universe," than to say, "thou exceedingly wishest to bear the universe." And in iii. 9, 3, where Sâyaṇa explains the words *ati tṛshṭam vavakshitha*, "thou (Agni) exceedingly wishest to bring, in order to fulfil the desire of thy worshipper, by bestowing an appropriate reward." Roth (*s. v. tṛshṭa*) proposes to render "thou (Agni) hast overcome that which bites, *i.e.* the smoke." Similarly, in ii. 22, 3; iv. 16, 5; viii. 77, 5, the sense of "waxing" seems by far the most appropriate (though not, apparently, in ii. 34, 4). Even in viii. 12, 25–27, where at first sight the meaning "carried" seems to suit the context,—"when, Indra, the gods placed thee in the front in the battle, then thy beautiful steeds *carried* (*thee*)",—the other sense, "grew great," would be admissible, especially as there is no noun in the line to be governed by *vavakshatuḥ*, and as in the next verse following the three where this verb occurs, another verb with that very signification (*vavṛdhâte*, "grew") is actually applied to the horses. Other forms of this verb, *vakshati* and *vakshatah*, occur in R.V. i. 2, 2; iv. 8, 2; viii. 6, 45; where they are treated by Sâyaṇa as futures, or precatives. Can *vakshati* be a third per. pres., "he brings?" *Âvakshat* and *vakshat* (R.V. x. 20, 10, and x. 176, 2) seem to have the sense of "bringing." *Vakshatha* occurs as a substantive in vii. 33, 8, where Sâyaṇa assigns the sense of *prakâṣa*, "brightness." Perhaps it may mean "full splendour." Roth (Illustr. of Nir. p. 30) thinks the root *vaksh* has the sense of "waxing;" so, too, Benfey (gloss to S.V.), who, however, gives it the sense of "carrying" in R.V. iv. 7, 11. In his translation of i. 64, 3; i. 81, 5; i. 102, 8, he translates "growing." Westergaard also *s.v.* adopts the sense of "growing," "being strong," etc.

Ṣarman has in the Nighaṇṭus, iii. 4, the sense of "house." In Nir. ix. 19, 32; xii. 45, it has the meaning of "refuge" (*ṣaraṇam*). In i. 174, 2, Sâyaṇa renders *ṣarma* by *sukhaṃ yathâ bhavati*, "easily," whilst in another verse, vi. 20, 10, where the context is the same, he translates it by "thunderbolt" (*ṣarma ṣarmaṇâ vajreṇa*).

Ṣârada, "autumnal," (which is not found in the Nirukta), is a word applied in several passages of the R.V. to the cities of the Dasyus. On i. 131, 4, Sâyaṇa explains it as = "fortified for a year;" on i. 174, 2, as "new," or "fortified for a year;" on vi. 20, 10, as "belonging to an Asura called Ṣarad."

Ṣurudh, in the plural, means, according to the Nirukta, vi. 16, "waters," which "prevent distress" (*ṣucham saṃrundhanti*). The word is mentioned in two other passages of the Nir. viz., x. 41 and xii. 18 (where R.V. iv. 23, 8, and vi. 49, 8, are cited), in the former of which no further explanation of it is given, whilst in the later (xii. 18) it is rendered by *dhanâni*, "riches." Sâyaṇa, on i. 72, 7, takes the word for "food which prevents suffering in the shape of hunger" (*kshudrûpasya sokasya rodhayitrîr ishaḥ*); on iii. 38, 5, for "preventives of thirst, waters;" on iv. 23, 8, for "waters;" on vi. 3, 3, for "preventives of suffering, cows;"[1] on vi. 49, 8 (=Nir. xii. 18) the same (in opposition to Yâska, who here renders it "riches"); on vii. 23, 2, for "things which prevent suffering, herbs;" and on vii. 62, 3, for "preventers of suffering," but taken as nom. masc. and as an epithet of Varuṇa and other gods; or, optionally, in the accus., for "plants." In i. 169, 8, the word is interpreted of "distress-preventing desiccating lines of clouds," *ṣokasya rodhayitrîḥ ṣoshakâḥ . . . . megha-panktîḥ*. R.V. vi. 49, 8, is repeated in the Vâj. S. xxxiv. 42, where *ṣurudhaḥ* is explained as "a means of removing suffering."

[1] These cows belong to the Râkshasas, whom Sâyaṇa considers to be denoted by the word *aktu*, "night," in which such spirits move about.

Salalûka is explained in Nir. vi. 3 (where the only text in which it occurs, R.V. iii. 30, 17, is cited), as="covetous (*saṃlubdha*), wicked, according to the Nairuktas, or etymologists; or it may be for *sararûka*, from *sṛ* (to go), reduplicated." Durga understands it to mean "confounded," or "fugitive," of the Râkshases. Sâyaṇa takes it for *saraṇa-śîla*, "moving."

Santya is found as an epithet of Agni in R.V. i. 18, 2; i. 36, 2; viii. 19, 26. In the first of these passages Sâyaṇa explains it as meaning "bestower of rewards," and in the second as "liberal," deriving it in both cases from the root *san*, "to give." In the third passage he makes it =*sambhajanîya*, "to be served, or possessed."

Sarvatâti is interpreted in Nir. xi. 24 (where R.V. i. 94, 15, is quoted) by *sarvâsu karma-tatishu*, "in all performances (*lit.* extensions) of works." Sâyaṇa on the same passage repeats these words of Yâska, and adds, "or to him who is present at all sacrifices." On iv. 26, 3, he translates it simply by "sacrifice." On vi. 12, 2, also, he renders it by "sacrifice" ("performed by all," *sarvais tâyamâne yajne*), or, (taking *tâti* for a suffix), the "totality" of worshippers (*sarvaḥ stotâ*). On i. 106, 2, he renders it by "that which is extended by all heroes, battle," which sense he also assigns to it in vii. 18, 19. On iii. 54, 11, he gives it the signification of "every desired good." In this last text, where Savitṛ is asked to give the worshippers *sarvatâti* (*âd asmabhyam âsuva sarvatâtim*), it could not well signify either battle, or sacrifice, or anything but blessing in some form or other. On vi. 56, 6, the scholiast assigns the sense of "sacrifice," or "the extension of all enjoyments," *sarveshâṃ bhogânâṃ vistârâya*. The word also occurs in ix. 96, 4; x. 36, 14; and x. 100, 1 ff., but Sâyaṇa's explanations of those passages are not within my reach. See Prof. Benfey's Excursus on the word *sarvatâti* in his "Orient und Occident," ii. 519 ff., referred to in my article on "Vedic Theogony," etc., p. 70, note.

Sumajjâni (not in the Nirukta), is an epithet of Vishṇu in R.V. i. 156, 2. Sâyaṇa thinks it may mean one of two things, either "self-born" (*sumat* being = *svayam* according to Nir. vi. 22, and *jâni* being taken for "birth"), or "having a wife (*jâni*) who gladdens" (*sumat* being here = *sutarâṃ mâdayati*). The epithet will in the latter case be equivalent to the "lord of the world-gladdening Ṣrî." Here we have an importation of later ideas into Vedic mythology. I am not aware of any other passage of the R.V. in which a wife is assigned to Vishṇu. In the Vâj. S. xxix. 60, Aditi is called his wife; as Sinîvâlî appears to be in A.V. vii. 46, 3.

Spaṣ, as a verb, is found in R.V. i. 10, 2. where Sâyaṇa translates it by "touched, began;" in i. 22, 19 (= Vâj. vi. 14; Sâma-veda, ii. 1021), where he renders it by "(every worshipper) touched, performed," the root *spaṣ* having the two senses of injuring and touching (*bâdhana-sparṣanayoḥ*). Mahîdhara on Vâj. S. vi. 4, explains the same word by "bound, fashioned," or "bound in himself," or "fixed," *spaṣ* having the sense of binding (*bandhane*). In i. 128, 4, Sâyaṇa translates by *atyarthaṃ spṛṣati svîkaroti*, "touches exceedingly, accepts," (the sense of "oblations, etc.," being given to *jâtâni*); in i. 176, 3, by *bâdhayasva*, "injure." The verb also occurs without a preposition in x. 102, 8, and with *anu* prefixed in x. 14, 1, and x. 160, 4. I am not aware what sense Sâyaṇa assigns in the first two passages, but in the third he translates *anuspashṭa* by *dṛshṭigochara*, "visible" (see Goldstücker's Dict. *s.v. aratni*). *Spaṣ*, as a noun, is found in R.V. i. 25, 13; i. 33. 8; iv. 4, 3; v. 59, 1; vi. 67, 5; vii. 61, 3; vii. 87, 3; viii. 50, 15; ix. 73, 4, 7; and A.V. iv. 16, 4. In the first passage Sâyaṇa renders it, *hiraṇya-sparṣino rasmîn*, "gold-touching, rays;" in the second (i. 33, 8), *bâdhakân Vṛttrânucharân*, "the injurious followers of Vṛttra;" in the third (iv. 4, 3) by *parabâdhakân raṣmîn chârân vâ*, "destroying others, rays, or spies;" in the fourth (vi. 67, 5) by "rays, or spies; in the fifth (vii. 61, 3)[1] by *rûpam*, "form;" in vii. 87, 3, by *charâḥ*, "spies," (though here, too, the root *spaṣ* is said to have the sense of *spṛṣ*, "touch.") In v. 59, 1, *spaṭ*, nom. sing., is said by the scholiast to be = *sprashṭâ hotâ*, "priest;" whilst in viii. 50, 15, where it is an epithet of Indra, he makes it mean *sarvasya jnâtâ*,

[1] In vii. 61, 3, there is another instance of Sâyaṇa's making a reference back to a preceding passage, i. 61, 9, See also his notes on i. 154, 1; ii. 2, 5; iii. 17, 1; vi. 26, 4; vii. 76, 4.

"knower of all things." The sense of the noun *spaṣ* is pretty well fixed by A.V. iv. 16, 4, to be generally that of spies or messengers. And I do not see why in some, at least, of the texts of the R.V. above quoted the verb too should not have the sense of "seeing," or "shewing." The root *spaṣ* has the significations of "making evident," "informing," given to it among others in Wilson's Dictionary. The participles *spashṭa* and *anuspashṭa*, "manifest," seem to come from a verb meaning "to see." *Spaṣ*, "a spy," also appears to be derived from a root having the same sense. And in the cognate languages the root has the same signification. See Roth's Illustrations of the Nirukta, p. 138 f.

Smaddishṭi, *smadishṭa*, are not to be found in the Nirukta. The former word (divided into *smad* + *dishṭi* in the Pada text) occurs several times in the R.V., viz., in iii. 45, 5, as an epithet of Indra, where Sâyaṇa translates it by *bhadra-vâkya*, "auspiciously speaking;" in vi. 63, 9, where he takes it for an epithet of chariots or horses, and renders it "handsome-looking," *praṣasta-darṣanân* (where *dishṭi* must be taken to stand for *dṛshṭi*); in vii. 18, 23, where it is an epithet of *dânâḥ*, "horses," and is explained by him as "possessing all the approved attributes of a gift, liberality, faith," etc. (*praṣastâti-sarjana-ṣraddhâdi-dânânga-yuktâḥ*). These interpretations seem to be mutually discrepant. His commentary on x. 62, 10, where the word is also found, is not accessible to me. The second word, *smadishṭa*, differs from the first, in that it ends not in *ṭi* but in *ṭa*, and is compounded of *smat* + *ishṭa*, occurs in R.V. vii. 87, 3, where Sâyaṇa renders it, "either good goers, or, sent together," according as *smat* is taken in the sense of "good," or "with."

Kuṇḍṛṇâchî is explained by Sâyaṇa on R.V. i. 29, 6, as denoting the tortuous movement of the wind; whilst in Vâj. S. 24, 35, as interpreted by Mahîdhara, it signifies some kind of wild animal. The words *prâvo yudhyantam ṛshabhaṃ daṣadyum* occur both in R.V. i. 33, 14, and in vi. 26, 4, but are differently explained by Sâyaṇa in these two places. In the former he renders, "thou hast preserved the eminent (rishi) Daṣadyu when fighting;" whilst in the latter he makes Vṛshabha a proper name and Daṣadyu an epithet, translating, "thou hast preserved (the king) Vṛshabha fighting for ten days." This discrepancy is pointed out by Prof. Benfey in his note 294 to the former text (Orient und Occident, i. p. 51), and he then proceeds: "I am far from imputing this to Sâyaṇa as an offence. He was as little aware of it as we are now. I make the remark only for the sake of those who attach so great importance to him that, instead of the Veda, they translate his Commentary, and while doing so, pretend to be giving a translation of the hymns."

Pṛshṭa in R.V. i. 98, 2, is explained by Sâyaṇa as meaning either *saṃspṛshṭa,* "touched," or *nishikṭa, nihita,* "shed, placed."

Prashṭi is explained by Sâyaṇa on R.V. i. 39, 6, as "a particular kind of yoke between the three animals which draw the chariot," *etat-sanjnako vâhana-traya-madhya-vartti yuga-viṣeshaḥ.* On viii. 7, 28, he takes *prashṭi* to mean either "swift," or "a buck yoked in front." See Prof. Wilson's note on the former passage. The words *puruṇîthâ jarasva* in R.V. vii. 9, 6, are interpreted by Sâyaṇa to mean either "praise with much laudation," or "consume the Râkshasas who move by many paths."

Gûrttaṣravas is explained by Sâyaṇa on i. 61, 5, as *praṣasyânna,* "having approved food;" and on i. 122, 10, as *ud-gûrṇa-dîpti, prakhyâtânno vâ,* "having exalted light," or "having renowned food."

Vîtahavya, in R.V. vi. 15, 2, is said by Sâyaṇa either to mean a rishi so called, or, if Bharadvâja be the rishi of the hymn, then *vîtahavya* will be an epithet signifying "he by whom an oblation has been presented." The word occurs again in vii. 19, 3, where the scholiast takes it for an epithet of Sudâs, meaning, "he who has given, or generated, an oblation."

Ṣvaitreya, which in R.V. i. 33, 14, is taken by Sâyaṇa for a proper name, the son of *Ṣvitrâ,* is in v. 19, 3, understood of the "lightning-fire produced in the atmosphere," although the word has the appearance of being a proper name in that passage also.

Akavâri is not in the Nirukta. It is found in R.V. iii. 47, 5, as an epithet of Indra, and is there explained by Sâyaṇa as =*prabhûta-ṣatrukam*, "having many enemies," or *akutsitârim*, "having foes not contemptible." The last sense he illustrates by a reference to R.V. i. 61, 9, where the epithet *svari*, "having glorious enemies," is applied to Indra, as implying that the vanquisher of such enemies must be most heroic. In vii. 96, 3, *akavârî* is spoken of Sarasvatî, and is interpreted in quite a different manner by Sâyaṇa, as *akutsita-gamanâ*, "not badly going." The first of the preceding verses is repeated in Vâj. S. vii. 36, where *akavâri* is taken as either "he whose enemies even are not bad," or "he who obtains what is not bad," *i.e.* "has eminent dominion."

Akshṇayâvan is not in the Nirukta, but is found in R.V. viii. 7, 35, where Sâyaṇa gives two explanations, viz., either "going pervadingly" (*vyâptaṃ gachhantaḥ*), or "going quicker than even the eye."

Ȧdha-priya, kadha-priya, kadha-prî. The first of these words occurs as an epithet of the Aṣvins in R.V. viii. 8, 4, where Sâyaṇa offers two interpretations, either (1) "fond of that which exists here *below*, viz., Soma," or (2) "fond of praise," *adha* standing for *kadha*, shorn of its initial *k*. Prof. Roth, *s.v.*, renders, "then pleased." Prof. Goldstücker does not give the word. *Kadha-priya* is found in R.V. i. 30, 20, as an epithet of Ushas, and *kadha-prî* in i. 38, 1, and viii. 7, 31, as an epithet of the Maruts, and both terms are uniformly rendered by Sâyaṇa "fond of praise," *kadha* being said to stand for *katha* or *kathâ*, "speaking." Prof. Roth, *s.vv.*, suggests, "friendly to whom?" And, certainly, when it is observed that all the three passages in which the two words are found are interrogative, this rendering seems more probable than Sâyaṇa's. Compare *kuhayâkṛte* in viii. 24, 30. Prof. Benfoy translates in i. 30, 20, "where lovest thou?" and in i. 38, 1, "where do ye like to linger?"

Anarviṣ. On this word it will be sufficient to quote Prof. Goldstücker's explanation in his Dictionary: "(*ved.*) i. A car-man, one going with, or on a cart." . . . "(or, according to another explanation, which appears, however, to be an artificial one), ii. one who does not arrive where he is to go to, one not attaining the end or aim of his journey." The artificial explanation here alluded to is that of Sâyaṇa on i. 121, 7.

Amavat is explained by Prof. Roth, *s.v.*, as "violent," "strong," etc.; and by Prof. Goldstücker, *s.v.*, "powerful, mighty, strong." The latter scholar remarks that "this meaning of *amavat* seems to apply satisfactorily to all other instances in which the word occurs. . . . . . There are, however, other meanings . . . . mentioned by Yâska, and accordingly by Sâyaṇa and Mahîdhara, which deserve noticing, not only because the first of them is plausible, but also on account of their high antiquity." The words of Yâska (vi. 12) explanatory of the word before us are *amâtyavân abhyamanavân svavân vâ, i.e.*, either "with ministers, or with diseases, or with riches." See Goldstücker, *s.vv. amavat* and *abhyamanavat*. Yâska seems thus to have been undecided as to the sense. See also Sâyaṇa on R.V. iv. 4, 1, and Wilson's note on the same passage, as also Mahîdhara on Vâj. S. 13, 9.

Amina is explained by Sâyaṇa on R.V. vi. 19, as=*ahiṃsanîya*, "uninjurable;" and on this passage he gives no other sense. Prof. Goldstücker, *s.v.*, after assigning the two senses (1) "of an unlimited measure or quantity (of strength), or (2) uninjured," goes on to say: "According to Yâska (vi. 16) the word may have either of these meanings in the following verse of the R.V. (vi. 19, 1);" and quotes Durga, the commentator on Yâska, to show that the words of the latter are to be so understood. Durga also observes that from the form of the word, and the suitableness of both senses, either is admissible. But we are not yet arrived at an end of the optional meanings proposed for this adjective. I learn from Prof. Goldstücker's next article that in another text (R.V. x. 116, 4), where this same term occurs (applied, too, as in vi. 19, 1, along with *dvibarhas*, as an epithet of Indra), it has two other meanings assigned to it by Sâyaṇa, *both different from those assigned by Yâska* to the word in R.V. vi. 19, 1 (and one of which he (Sâyaṇa) himself adopts in his note on that passage). These two new meanings are "going everywhere" (*sarvayantâ*), and "all-beloved" (*sarvaiḥ kâmyamânaḥ*).

Could anything show more demonstratively the conjectural and etymological character of many of Sâyaṇa's interpretations?

Amatra is found as an epithet of Indra in R.V. i. 61, 9, where it is explained by Sâyaṇa as either = "expert in moving in battles, etc., or devoid of any limit." It is also found in iii. 36, 4, where the Commentator renders it, "a vanquisher of enemies." This latter text is quoted in Nir. vi. 23, where the senses of "measureless, great, or uninjured," are assigned to the word. See Goldstücker, *s.v. abhyamita*.

Amitavarṇa, spoken of the Dawns in R.V. iv. 51, 9, is explained by Sâyaṇa as = *ahiṃsitavarṇâ aparimitavarṇâ vâ*, "either of uninjured colour, or of unlimited colour." He could not therefore have had any precise idea of the sense.

Amanda, applied to hymns in R.V. i. 126, 1, is by Yâska, (ix. 10) in his explanation of that passage, rendered as = *abâliṣân analpân vâ*, "either not foolish, or not few." Sâyaṇa contents himself with the second sense.

Ayâsya has more than one signification assigned to it by Sâyaṇa in i. 62, 7, and viii. 51, 2. See Prof. Goldstücker's Dictionary, *s.v.*

Aptur, said to be derived from *ap*, "water," and *tur*, "to hasten," an epithet of the gods in general (R.V. i. 3, 8), of Agni (iii. 27, 11), of Indra (iii. 51, 2, and according to the scholiast, in ii. 21, 5 also, though there it may be a nom. pl.), is declared by Sâyaṇa to have in all these passages the sense of "sender, or senders, of water." In i. 118, 4, where it is an epithet of the horses (according to Sâyaṇa), or the falcons, of the Aṣvins, he ascribes to it the signification of "quick like the waters" (*âpa iva tvaropetâḥ*). Prof. Goldstücker follows the Scholiast in assigning to it both these senses, viz.: "(1) sending water (*i.e.* rain), an epithet of Indra, Agni, etc.; (2) quick as water (*i.e.* as the falling rain), an epithet of the horses of the Aṣwins." I confess I do not think the commentator's opinion a sufficient reason for concluding that the word has two different meanings. It also occurs in R.V. ix. 61, 13 = S.V. i. 487, where Prof. Benfey renders it "flood-conquering" (while in his Glossary he makes it "water-shedding"). In his translation of R.V. i. 3, 8, in Orient und Occident, he gives it the sense of "active in works," and in i. 118, 4, of "hastening through the air." Prof. Roth, in his Lexicon, *s.v.*, renders it "active, zealous." The substantive *aptûryam* is rendered with some variation by Sâyaṇa in two passages, R.V. iii. 12, 8, and iii. 51, 9, as *vṛshṭi-dvârâ prerakatvam,* "the quality of impelling (or stimulating) *by means of* rain," and *apâm preraṇe,* "in the impelling (or sending) of rain."

In R.V. iii. 27, 11, the word *yanturam,* an epithet of Agni, is explained as either = *sarvasya niyantâram,* "the controuler of all things," or *kshipraṃ gantâram,* "quickly going."

Ardhadeva, in R.V. iv. 42, 8, is interpreted by Sâyaṇa as either "near the gods," or "half a god."

Asaṣchat is a participle of frequent occurrence in the R.V. One of the passages in which it is found, vi. 70, 2, is quoted in Nir. v. 2, where it is said to be equivalent to *asajyamâne,* "not attached together," or *vyudasyantyau,* "throwing apart, scattering." Sâyaṇa on this verse merely repeats Yâska. In i. 160, 2, where the word is again an epithet of heaven and earth, he explains it similarly, *asajyamâne paraspara-viyukte,* "not attached, separate from each other." In i. 112, 2, he takes it for an epithet of the worshippers, in the sense of *anyatrânâsaktâḥ,* "not attached to any one else." In vii. 67, 9, it is an epithet of the Aṣvins, and is in like manner interpreted by him *kutrâpy asajyamânau,* "not attached anywhere. In iii. 57, 6, he connects it with *pramati,* "the design" or "disposition" of Agni, derives it from *saṣch,* "to go," and explains it *asmad anyatra sangatim akurvâṇâ,* "not forming an union with any one but us." In. ii. 32, 3, it is an epithet of *dhenu,* "cow," and he there renders it *asaktâvayavâm,* "having her members unattached" (to what?). In ii. 25, 4, where he regards it as an epithet of "waters," (understood), he explains it, *asajyamânâḥ, aniruddhâḥ,* "unattached, unobstructed." In viii. 31, 4, where it is an epithet of *iḷâ,* "food," he derives it from *saṣch,* "to go," and renders it by *ăgamana-ṣîlam,,* "that whose character is not to go, or depart." In i. 13, 6, and i. 142, 6 (two verses which are partly identical in contents), the word *asaṣchataḥ* is an epithet of *dvârah*, "doors." In the former of the two texts (i. 13, 6), Sâyaṇa renders it *udghâṭanena praveshtṛ-purusha-sanga-rahitâḥ*, "destitute of the contact or presence of persons entering in consequence of their being opened" (*i.e.* as Prof. Wilson explains "[hitherto] unentered"); whilst in the second passage (i. 142, 6) he renders *asajyamânâḥ paraspara-viprakṛshṭâḥ*,[1] "not attached or joined, distant or apart from each other." The renderings in the last two (parallel) passages seem to be mutually inconsistent, as the latter appears to mean that the doors, of which the two halves stood apart, were open, whilst the former, although we adopt Prof. Wilson's addition of "hitherto," imports that although they were about to be opened, they were still closed. In i. 13, 6, Rosen translates, "non frequentatæ" (which does not differ materially from Wilson's rendering); but in his note, subsequently composed, he says he should (in addition to other changes) prefer to interpret the word under consideration "non clausæ." I observe that in the quotation which he there adduces from Sâyaṇa's Commentary, his reading differs from that given by Müller, in adding a negative particle, as it runs thus, *udghâṭanena na purusha-sanga-rahitâḥ*, which would make the sense, "doors which from their being opened are *not* destitute of the contact or presence of persons entering." Westergaard, *s.v. saṣch*, follows Rosen's note in rendering *asaṣchataḥ* by "portæ non clausæ." Sâyaṇa, on i. 13, 6, derives the word from *sasj*, "to go," with *a* negative prefixed, but in the passages where he renders it by *asajyamâna*, or *anâsakta*, "not attached," he must, I suppose, be understood to ascribe to this root the sense of "being joined, or attached." Wilson, in his note on i. 142, 6, has noticed the variations in Sâyaṇa's rendering of the term *asaṣchataḥ*. In addition to this discrepancy between his translations of i. 13, 6 and i. 142, 6, I have to observe that Sâyaṇa's explanation of the word in viii. 31, 4, as meaning "that which does not depart," seems to be scarcely consistent

[1] I should add that Sâyaṇa here offers alternative renderings both of *asaṣchataḥ*—making it a masc. pl. with the sense, "devoid of persons entering,"—and of the verb *viṣrayantâm*, which he says may be explained not only "let them be opened," but "let them seek, or approach" (*sevantâm*).

with the signification "unobstructed," which he assigns in ii. 25, 4, which implies that the waters could depart elsewhere. At all events, the two meanings are quite different. I have no access to Sâyaṇa's explanations of the word where it occurs in the ninth and tenth books of the R.V.; but R.V. ix. 57, 1, is repeated in the Sâma-veda, ii. 1111, where I find from Prof. Benfey's Glossary that the Scholiast renders it *sanga-rahita*, "free from contact." Benfey himself, in his Glossary, translates it "free from pursuers, unhindered," or, when spoken of rain, "thick." In his translation of the passage of the S.V. however, he renders the word by "lovely;" and the cognate word *asaşchushî* in S.V. ii. 502, by "kindly-disposed." In his translation of R.V. i. 13, 6, in Orient und Occident, Benfey renders *asaşchataḥ*, "good" (from *a* privative and *saşchat*, "persecuting, enemy"); but in i. 112, 2, he gives "inexhaustible" (unversiegbar) as its equivalent. Prof. Roth (see his Lexicon, *s.v.*) proposes to render "unfailing." On the whole I think that the senses proposed by Sâyaṇa are either too various, too vague, or two forced, to be admitted as satisfactory, and have very much the appearance of being conjectural.

Âhanas is understood by Yâska (iv. 15, in his interpretation of R.V. ix. 75, 5, where it occurs in the plural as an epithet of *madâḥ*, "intoxicating draughts"), as = *âhananavantaḥ*, "smiting." In his explanation (Nir. v. 2) of R.V. x. 10, 8, where it is an epithet of Yamî, he adheres to the same etymology, and makes it signify "smiting as it were with uncivil words" (*âhamsîva bhâshamâṇâ iti asabhya-bhâshaṇâd ahanâ iva bhavati etasmâd âhanaḥ syât*). I have not access to Sâyaṇa's Commentary on these two verses, or on x. 125, 2; but on ii. 13, 1 (where he applies it to Soma) he takes it in a passive sense, "to be smitten, to be poured out" (*âhantavyo 'bhishotavyaḥ*), while on v. 42, 13, he gives it the active signification of *âhantâ sektâ*, "smiter, shedder." It seems unlikely that the term should have both these senses.

Âtuje in R.V. vii. 32, 9, is explained by Sâyaṇa as an epithet (in the dative) of Indra, with the meaning either "of destroyer of enemies, or giver of wealth." Müller makes it mean "to give." The last words of the verse, *na devâsaḥ kavatnave*, are rendered by Müller (Anc. Sansk. Lit. p. 544), "the gods are not to be trifled with." Wilson has, "the gods favour not the imperfect rite." In his note he shows a curious misapprehension of Sâyaṇa when he says: "The scholiast seems to render it, men do not become gods by such means, *devâ na bhavanti.*" These last words merely mean, as I take them: "The gods are not for (*i.e.*, are not favourers of) a *kavatnu*;" whether that adjective means, as Roth, *s.v.*, proposes, "a niggard," or, possibly,—as may be suggested, if we regard it as in opposition to the word *taraṇi* in the preceding clause,—"an inert or timid man." In illustration of the construction, compare iv. 33, 11, *na ṛte ṣrântasya sakhyâya devâḥ*, "the gods [are not disposed] for the friendship of the man who is tired of sacred rites" (though Sâyaṇa renders differently); and vii. 61, 5, *na vâṃ niṇyâny achite abhûvan*, "your secret things are not for the unthinking man." (Wilson does not translate Sâyaṇa accurately here).

In R.V. i. 84, 16, Sâyaṇa assigns to the word *kaḥ* the optional senses of "who?" or of "Prajâpati," and to *gâḥ* those of "horses," or "words of the Veda."

Dhiyâvasu is an epithet of Sarasvatî in i. 3, 10 (=Vâj. S. 20, 84), and of Agni in iii. 3, 2, and iii. 28, 1. Yâska comments on the first of these passages in Nir. xi. 26, and there explains *dhiyâvasu* by the vague equivalent *karmavasu*, which may mean, "rich in works," or "she who through works confers wealth." This last sense, though not in itself obvious, is the one extracted from the compound by Sâyaṇa, who render *skarma-prâpya-dhana-nimitta-bhûtâ*, "she who is the cause of the wealth which is to be acquired through works." He afterwards repeats the same explanation in the words, *dhiyâ karmaṇâ vasu yasyâḥ sukâṣâd bhavati sâ dhiyâvasuḥ.* On iii. 28, 1 he interprets similarly, and Mahîdhara on Vâj. S. 20, 84, not very differently. On R.V. iii. 3, 2, however, Sâyaṇa gives the word a totally different sense, *prajnayâ vyâptaḥ*, "pervaded by wisdom."

Vidadvasu is variously explained by Sâyaṇa in three different passages, i. 6, 6; v. 39, 1; viii. 55, 1. In the first, where he takes it for an epithet of the Maruts, he makes it signify *vedayadbhiḥ sva-mahima-prakhyâpakair vasubhir dhanair yuktam,* "possessed of riches which make known their greatness." Further on he gives the additional explanation, *audâryâtiṣayavattayâ jnâpayanti vasûni dhanâni yaṃ sa vidadvasuḥ,* "he whom his riches make known as exceedingly generous is *vidadvsau.*" In v. 39, 1, the word is applied to Indra, and there the Scholiast gives it the sense of *labdha-dhana,* "he by whom wealth has been obtained."[1] In viii. 55, 1, where it is an epithet of the same god, it is declared by Sâyaṇa to mean *vedayadvasuṃ dhanâvedakam,* the god "who makes known riches." The term, however, was most probably intended by the authors of the hymns to have but one sense.

Gabhasti, in R.V. i. 54, 4, is interpreted by Sâyaṇa as either "taken with the hand," or "having rays."

Hvârya, in R.V. v. 9, 4, receives from Sâyaṇa a threefold interpretation, viz. either (1) "a wriggling serpent," or (2) "a horse performing the *âskandita* and other tortuous movements," or (3) "an unbroken colt." Compare Wilson's note.

Kaṣâ means a "whip," but in the Nighaṇṭus i. 11, it is also said to be one of the fifty-six synonymes of *vâch,* "speech." In R.V. i. 22, 3, and i. 157, 4, mention is made of the *kaṣâ madhumatî* or "honied whip" of the Aṣvins, and they are asked to moisten with it the sacrifice or the worshippers. In both these places Sâyaṇa gives an optional rendering of *kaṣâ,* as signifying either "whip," or "speech." Mahîdhara on Vâj. S. 7, 11, gives the word the sense of "speech" only. See Note 1 in p. 363 of my Article on the "Progress of the Vedic Religion," etc., in the last volume of this Journal.

Krandasî is interpreted by Sâyaṇa on R.V. ii. 12, 8, as either "heaven and earth making a sound," or "two armies, human and divine." On vi. 25, 4, he takes it for two disputants "crying and abusing" each other (*krandamânâv âkroṣantau*). I have not access to his commentary on x.

[1] Yâska quotes this verse (Nir. iv. 4) and explains *vidadvasu* by *vittadhana,* which may mean either "he by whom wealth is known," or "by whom wealth has been obtained."

121, 6, but I observe that Prof. Müller in his translation of the hymn (Anc. Sansk. Lit., p. 569) renders the term by "heaven and earth," which is also the only sense assigned to it by Mahîdhara on Vâj. S. 32, 7, where the verse is repeated.

Nabhanya is explained by Sâyaṇa in i. 149, 3, as = *nabhasi bhavo nabhasvân vâyuḥ*, "that which is produced, or exists, in the sky, the wind;" in i. 173, 1, as = *nabhasyaṃ nabhasi bhavaṃ nabhovyâpinaṃ hiṃsakaṃ vâ râkshasâdikasya*, either "etherial, pervading the sky," or "destructive of Râkshasas," etc.; and in vii. 42, 1, as = *stotra*, "a hymn."

Nṛchakshas, which is not in the Nirukta, is generally translated by Sâyaṇa, "beholder of men" (R.V. iv. 3, 3; vii. 60, 2), or, "beholder of the conductors of rites" (*nṛṇâm* being taken as = *karma-netṝṇâm*). In i. 22, 7, however, though said to mean primarily, "he who sees men" (*nṝnṣ chashṭe*), it is (as an epithet of Savitri) explained by the words, "illuminator of men" (*manushyâṇâm prkaâṣa-kâriṇam*); and in i. 91, 2, by "he who shows to the conductors of sacrifices the desired fruit (of their rites)."

Sûrachakshas is found in Nir. xi. 16 (where R.V. i. 110, 4, is explained) as an epithet of the Ribhus. Yâska gives it the sense of "sun-speaking (?) or sun-wise," *sûra-khyânâ vâ sûra-prajnâ vâ*. Sâyaṇa does not adhere to more than one of Yâska's renderings, and proposes *sûrya-samâna-prakâṣâḥ sûrya-sadṛṣa-jnânâ vâ*, "having splendour like the sun," or "having knowledge like the sun." The word also occurs in R.V. i. 16, 1, where Sâyaṇa takes it for *sûrya-samâna-prakâṣa-yuktâ ṛtvijaḥ*, "having splendour like the sun, priests." The correctness of this last interpretation seems very doubtful; and I do not see why the word should not be, as Benfey makes it (Or. und Occ.), an epithet of *harayaḥ*, Indra's tawny horses. If so, the verse would run thus: "Let the tawny horses bring thee, the vigorous, to the soma-draught, Indra, thee, the sun-eyed steeds." The sense of "eye" or "sight" is assigned by Sâyaṇa in v. 66, 6, to *chakshas* in *tya-chakshasâ*, which he renders *vyâpta-darṣanau*; in *sahasra-chakshas*, an epithet of Varuṇa, in vii. 34, 10, which he interprets by *bahu-chakshus*, "many-eyed;" and, optionally, in the compound *ghora-chak-*

shase (vii. 104, 2), which he explains *ghora-darṣanâya parusha-bhâshiṇe vâ*. *Sûrachakshas* is rendered "sun-eyed" by Benfey in i. 116, 4, also; though in his note he doubts whether this means, "with eyes gleaming like the sun," or "with eyes which see all, like the sun." To the compound *uruchakshas*, Sâyaṇa gives the sense of "seer of many," in i. 25, 5, and vii. 51, 9; of "great seers," in viii. 90, 2; of "to be seen by many," in i. 25, 16; but of "possessing great brilliancy," in vii. 35, 8; vii. 63, 4.

Châkshma, in R.V. ii. 24, 9, is said by Sâyaṇa to signify *sarvasya drashṭâ sarva-saho vâ*, either "all-seeing," or "all-enduring."

Jenya is explained by Sâyaṇa on R.V. i. 74, 4, as meaning either "manifested," or "conquerors (of Râkshasas)."

Pastyâ, though generally rendered by Sâyaṇa "people," "men," house," "dwellers in a house" (i. 25, 10; i. 40, 7; i. 164, 30), has in one place (iv. 1, 11) the alternative sense of "river" assigned to it.

In R.V. i. 180, 7, the words *vi paṇir hitavân* are said by Sâyaṇa to mean either, "the vessel which receives the stipulated libation (?) has had the liquid put into it" (*paṇiḥ paṇâdhâro droṇa-kalaṣo vihitavân sthâpita-rasavân âsît*), or "let the trafficker, avaricious, unsacrificing, who, though possessed of wealth, does not sacrifice, be separated" (*paṇir vaṇik lubdhako 'yashṭâ hitavân niyata-dhano dhanâḍhyo 'py ayashṭâ vi yujyatâm*). The difference between these two explanations is evidently prodigious, and shows how greatly the Scholiast was at a loss. Compare Wilson's note *in loco*.

Ûtayaḥ, generally rendered "aids," is in i. 84, 20, explained by Sâyaṇa as = *gantâraḥ* "goers," or as standing (with the loss of the initial *dh*) for *dhûtayaḥ*, "shakers," meaning the Maruts. He also assigns to *râdhâṃsi* in the same verse the unusual sense of "spirits" (*bhûtâni*). He seems to have regarded these strange interpretations as necessitated by the following verb *dabhan*, which has commonly the sense of "injure," "destroy." But it may have here, as Roth proposes, *s.v.*, the signification of "fail."

Dhṛta-vrata is an epithet often applied to the gods, chiefly to Mitra, Varuṇa, and the Âdityas. It means, "one whose ordinance stands fast," "one by whom the order of nature is upheld," according to Roth, *s.v.*, and Müller, "Anc. Sansk. Lit." p. 534. Sâyana on R.V. i. 15, 6, renders it by *svîkṛta-karmâṇau*, "those by whom works are accepted;" or, as Wilson translates, "propitious to pious acts." In i. 25, 8, also, Sâyaṇa explains the word *svîkṛta-karma-viṣeshaḥ*, "he by whom a particular work is accepted;"[1] whereas Müller (p. 536) makes it, "the upholder of order." In v. 1 of the same hymn the word *vrata* (with which *dhṛta-vrata* is compounded) is vaguely rendered by Sâyaṇa as = *karma*, "work;" and Wilson translates the phrase *vrataṃ praminîmasi* (which Sâyaṇa explains as = *karma pramâdena hiṃsitavantaḥ*), by "we disfigure thy worship by imperfections." Müller renders it, probably more accurately, "break thy laws." It is not clear which of the senses Sâyaṇa adopted; for in other passages, where there can be no doubt that the sense is what Müller makes it, Sâyaṇa uses the same terms of explanation. This is the case in ii. 38, 7, and v. 69, 4, where it is declared that no one can, or that the other gods cannot, hinder the ordinances of Savitri, or of Mitra and Varuna, in which passages it is far more likely that "decrees" or "designs," than "ceremonies," are contemplated. In ii. 28, 8, where it is said that the ordinances of Varuṇa rest unshaken on him as on a mountain, Sâyaṇa explains *vratâni* by *karmâṇi vidharaṇâni*, "works," "upholdings." And in ii. 38, 2, 9, he interprets the word of the "creative or impulsive act," *prasavâkhyaṃ karma*, of Savitri. So, too, in i. 101, 3, he gives it the signification of *niyama-rûpe karmaṇi*, *niyamanam* "controuling act," "controul;" in iii. 30, 4, of *karmaṇe*, *âjnâyai*, "command;" and in vii. 31, 11, of *rakshaṇâdîni karmâṇi*, "preservation and other works." But there are other passages in which he undoubtedly explains *vrata* by "rite," in accordance with the modern use of the word; as in i. 69, 4, where he takes it for *etâni paridṛṣyamânâni darṣa-pûrṇamâsâdîni karmâṇi*, "these rites which we see, the *darṣa*, *pûrṇamâsa*," etc.; and in i. 91, 3, where he takes it alternatively for *sarvâṇy agnishṭomâdîni karmâṇi*, "all the ceremonies, the

[1] On iv. 53, 4, he makes it = *dhṛtakarmâ*, "he by whom work is upheld."

agnishṭoma," etc., or *karmâṇi lokahitakârîṇi,* "acts promotive of the good of the world;" whilst in v. 63, 7, where Mitra and Varuṇa are said to uphold ordinances by their support, "through the wisdom of the divine Spirit," (*dharmaṇâ vratâ rakshethe asurasya mâyayâ*), he explains these words by *jagad-dhârakena vṛshṭy-âdi-lakshaṇena karmaṇâ vratâ yajnâdi-karmâṇi rakshethe pâlayathaḥ,* "ye support sacrifice and other rites by your world-sustaining action in the form of rain," etc. He interprets the word *vrata* in a similar manner in the following texts: i. 92, 12; i. 124, 2; ii. 28, 2; vii. 47, 3; vii. 76, 5. In most, at least, of these passages, however, there is little doubt the word *vrata* means "ordinances," or "laws." If there could be any question as to its having this meaning elsewhere, the point would be settled by R.V. x. 33, 9, *na devânâm ati vratam ṣatâtmâ chana jîvati,* "even the man of a hundred years does not live beyond the ordinance of (the term ordained by) the gods."[1] *Avrata* probably means quite as much "lawless," as "destitute of rites." (See Roth's Lexicon, *s.v.*) In x. 2, 4, where it is said that Agni rectifies whatever transgressions of the ordinances (*vratâni*) of the gods may be committed by the worshippers, the word probably alludes to sacred rites.

Raṇva in R.V. ii. 24, 11, means, Sâyaṇa tells us, *ramayitâ stotavyo vâ,* either "a giver of pleasure," or "one who is to be praised."

Râti in R.V. i. 60, 1, is a word about which Sâyaṇa is uncertain. He first explains it as "friend," a sense which he supports by the authority of Kapardin (whoever he may be), and then adds, "some say *râti* means "son," and in proof of this he quotes R.V. iii. 2. 4. But when we turn to that passage we find, strangely enough, that he renders the word by *abhilashitârthapradâtâram,* "giver of desired objects."

Rudravarttani, hiraṇyavarttani are epithets frequently applied to the gods, but diversely interpreted by Sâyaṇa. He explains the former in R.V. i. 3, 3, as meaning "leading in

[1] Compare R.V. viii. 28, 4, where a similar idea is expressed without the employment of the word *vrata: Yathâ vaṣanti devâs tathâ id asat tad eshâm nakir â minat,* etc., "As the gods wish, so it comes to pass; no one hinders that [will] of theirs," etc.

the front of the battle like heroes, who make their enemies weep." On viii. 22, 1, and 14, he renders it "those who in battle pursue a path characterized by weeping, or those whose path is praised." *Hiraṇyavarttani* in viii. 5, 11, he translates "they whose path is golden, or whose car is golden, or whose conduct is beneficent and pleasant" (*hita-ramaṇîyâcharaṇau.* On viii. 8, 1, he confines himself to the two latter senses. In vi. 61, 7, he makes it "having a golden chariot," and in viii. 26, 18, "having a golden path." Compare *kṛshṇa-varttani* and *ghṛtavarttani.*

Stṛbhiḥ is a word which Sâyaṇa translates by "stars" (*nakshatraiḥ*) in i. 68, 5; iv. 7, 3; vi. 49, 3, 12. Compare x. 68, 11. It is also found in ix. 68, 4, but I am not aware how he renders it there. Yâska explains the word in the same way, referring to one of these passages, iv. 7, 3, in illustration. In i. 87, 1, however, where it occurs in the following connection, *anjibhir vyânajre kechid usrâ iva stṛbhiḥ,* Sâyaṇa explains it by *svaṣarîrasyâchhâdakaiḥ,* "covering their bodies," a sense, which I suppose to be a purely conjectural one, based only on etymology. He separates it from its more immediate context and makes it an epithet of *anjibhiḥ,* rendering the clause thus: "The Maruts are seen distinct in the sky through the ornaments covering their bodies, like any rays of the sun shining in the sky." The position of *stṛbhiḥ* after *usrâḥ* is, however, rather adverse to this construction and rendering; and makes Roth's translation more probable, viz., "like many oxen with stars, *i.e.* white spots." See s. v. *usra.* Benfey translates differently, but retains the sense "stars," and thinks spots on the forehead may be meant. See Orient und Occident, ii. 250.

Sahasramushka is translated by Sâyaṇa on R.V. vi. 46, 3, (= Sâma-veda i. 286) as equivalent to *sahasraṣepha,* "mille membra genitalia habens;" and a story illustrative of Indra's lasciviousness is adduced from the Kaushîtakins to support this sense. In viii. 19, 32 the word is applied to Agni, and there Sâyaṇa renders it *bahutejaskam* "having many flames," *mushka* being considered as = *tejas,* from its stealing away, or removing darkness.

Sundhyu in R.V. i. 124, 4 is understood by Yâska (iv. 16) of the "sun," or of a "white water-fowl." Sâyaṇa repeats the same optional interpretation.

Svarâj, as an epithet of Indra, is differently explained by Sâyaṇa in R.V. 1, 61, 9; iii. 46, 1; vii. 82, 2; and viii. 12, 14. In iii. 46, 1, he makes it = *dhanâdhipati*, "lord of wealth," (*sva* here standing for "property"), and in the other places = *svenaiva tejasâ râjamâṇaḥ*, "shining by his own lustre," or *svayam eva anya-nirapekshayaiva râjamâṇaḥ*, "shining of himself, without reference to any one else," etc. In ii. 28, 1, where it is an epithet of Varuṇa, it is said by Sâyaṇa to mean "shining of himself," or "lord."

Sakshaṇi is differently explained by Sayaṇa in R.V. i. 111, 3, and in ii. 31, 4. In the former place it is said to mean "overcoming" (*asmân abhibhavantam*), whilst in the latter it is rendered, "to be served or reverenced" (*sachantyaḥ sevyaḥ*). In viii. 22, 15, also, it is similarly interpreted *sachantya-ṣîlau*. The word is also found in R.V. ix. 71, 4, and ix. 110, 1, but I have no access to the commentary on these two passages. The latter is, however, repeated in the Sâma-veda, i. 428, where Prof. Benfey renders the word "taming (enemies)." The sense of "overcoming" or "controuling" seems generally suitable in these passages. The word is, I presume, to be derived from the root *sah*, not from *sach*.

R.V. i. 140, 9. The word *tuvigrebhiḥ*, an epithet of Agni's attendants (*satvabhiḥ*) is explained by Sâyaṇa to mean either *prabhûtam ṣabdayadbhiḥ*, "much-sounding," or *prabhûta-gamanaiḥ*, "much-going." The apparently kindred word *tuvigraye*, R.V. ii. 21, 2 (an epithet, in the dative, of Indra) is said by him to mean either *pûrṇa-grîvâya*, "with full neck," or *bahubhiḥ stotavyâya*, "to be praised by many."

Vṛtaṇchaya, an epithet of Indra in R.V. ii. 21, 3, is declared by Sâyaṇa to mean either *abhîshṭasyâchetâ sanchetâ dâtâ*, "the bestower of what is desired," or (*vṛt ṣatruḥ, taṃ chayate hinasti iti vṛtanchayaḥ*, a "destroyer of enemies." *Radhrachoda*, in the following verse, is asserted to signify *samṛddhânâṃ prerakaḥ yadvâ hiṃsakânâṃ ṣatrûṇâṃ chodakaḥ*, either "a promoter of the affluent, or a driver of enemies."

Varûtrî appears to be explained by Sâyaṇa in i. 22, 10, as an epithet (*varaṇîya*, "to be desired"), of Dhishaṇâ, the goddess of speech. In vii. 38, 5, and vii. 40, 6, however, the word is treated as a proper name, denoting the goddess of speech, *Vâg-devî* or *Sarasvatî*. In Vâj. S. xi. 61, we have the word in the plural, *Varûtrîḥ*, where Mahîdhara says they are "goddesses personifying day and night" (*Varûtrayo devyo 'horâtrâbhimâninyaḥ* . . . "*ahorâtrâṇi vai varûtrayaḥ* | *ahorâtrair hi idaṃ sarvaṃ vṛtam*" *iti* (Ṣ. P. Br. 6, 5, 4, 6). In R.V. i. 22, 11, the epithet *achhinnapatra* is applied to the wives of the gods, and signifies, according to Sâyaṇa, "with wings uncut." For, he adds, "the wings of the wives of the gods, who have a winged form, are not cut by any one." Mahîdhara on Vâj. S. xi. 61, explains the term somewhat differently, as "those whose course or flight is not cut or hindered, constantly going," *achhinnam patram patanaṃ yâsâṃ tâḥ satatayâyinyaḥ*.

Vihâyas means, in modern Sanskrit, "sky," "bird." In the Nighaṇṭus 3, 3, it is given as one of the synonymes of *mahat*, "great." In Nir. iv. 15 (where Yâska quotes and interprets R.V. ix. 75, 5) it is said, as an epithet of *madâḥ*, "intoxicating draughts," to signify *vanchanavantaḥ*, "deceiving, deluding." The word occurs again as an epithet of Viṣvakarman in R.V. x. 72, 2 (=Vâj. S. 17, 26); and in Nir. x. 26, where that verse is explained, it is rendered by *vyâptâ*, "pervader." Mahîdhara interprets it as meaning either, "pervading like the ether," or "one who especially forsakes, a destroyer," *nabho-vad vyâpako yadvâ viṣesheṇa jahâti tyajati vihâyâḥ sanharttâ*. *Vihâyas* is also found as an epithet of Indra in R.V. iii. 36, 2, where Sâyaṇa, after stating that its constituent elements mean "the giver of the desired objects to suppliants," ends by assigning to it the simple sense of "great." (*vijahâty utsṛjaty arthân arthibhya iti vihâyâ mahân*. In iv. 11, 4, without entering into any explanation, he ascribes to it the same meaning. In his above cited comment on R.V. x. 72, 2 (Nir. x. 26), Yâska proposes no less than five different renderings for the participle *ishṭâni*, viz., *kântâni*, *krântâni*, *gatâni*, *matâni*, and *natâni*.

Vishitashṭukâ, an epithet of Rodasî ("the wife [of the Maruts, or lightning," *Marutpatnî vidyud vâ*) in R.V. i. 167, 5, is said by Sâyaṇa to mean either "having a distinguished mass of hair," or "having a dishevelled mass of hair" (*viśishṭa-keśa-sanghâ viprakîrṇa-keśa-sanghâ vâ*). Compare the different senses assigned to the word *pṛthushṭuka*, above.

Mesha occurs in the R.V. as a designation of Indra. On i. 51, 1 (=S.V. i. 376) Sâyaṇa renders it "striving with enemies, or ram, because Indra had come in that form to the rishi Medhâtithi when sacrificing, and drunk his soma," etc. On i. 52, 1 (=S.V. i. 377) the Scholiast only mentions the first of these two senses; but on viii. 86, 12, he returns to the second and gives it as the exclusive meaning. He here, however, says that Indra, in the form of a ram, carried Medhâtithi to heaven. In fact, there is a verse of the R.V. viii. 2, 40, which says, *itthâ dhîvantam adrivah Kâṇvam Medhyâtithim* | *mesho bhûto 'bhi yann ayaḥ* | "Thus, thunderer, having become a ram, and approaching the devout Medhyâtithi of the race of Kaṇva, thou didst carry him away, (or, thou didst depart)." Sâyaṇa gives to the verb *ayaḥ* here the causal sense of *agamayaḥ*. Compare the words of i. 51, 13, *menâ abhavo Vṛshaṇaśvasya*, which either arose out of, or gave rise to, another story about Indra.

Varîmabhiḥ, in R.V. i. 55, 2, is rendered by Sâyaṇa either "coverings, or vastnesses," *saṁvaraṇair yadvâ urutvaiḥ*.

In regard to *ubhayâsaḥ*, in R.V. i. 60, 2, it is left doubtful by Sâyaṇa, whether it means both gods and men, or priests and those for whom they officiated.

Varâha is given in Nigh. i. 10, as one of the names for "cloud." In Nir. v. 4, two senses, "cloud" and "boar," are assigned to it, R.V. i. 61, 7 being quoted as a passage where it has the former meaning. Sâyaṇa, *in loco*, understands it either of "cloud" or "sacrifice." See Wilson's note.

The notes to the fourth volume of Prof. Wilson's translation of the Rig-veda (verified by reference to the original Commentary), and an examination of parts of the volume itself, supply the following additional instances of double renderings by Sâyaṇa, or of variations in interpretation between him and Mahîdhara, the commentator on the Vâjasaneyi Sanhitâ:—

R.V. vi. 62, 8. *Rakshoyuje* is explained by Sâyaṇa as "lord or instigator of Rakshases, or priest united with Rakshases;"

ibid. 10. *Nṛvatâ rathena,* as "chariot with a charioteer, or with horses;"

vi. 63, 8. *Dhenum isham,* as "gladdening food, or desirable cow."

vi. 71, 3. *Hiraṇyajihva,* "golden-tongued" (so rendered by Wilson), is explained by Sâyaṇa as "having a kind, pleasant voice," though in the next verse he translates *hiraṇyapâṇi,* "golden-handed."

In vi. 75, 11 (=Vâj. S. xxix. 48) the tooth of an arrow is said to be *mṛga,* which Sâyaṇa (following Yâska, ix. 19) understands either as meaning that it is made of "deer's horn," or that it "searches out the enemy." Mahîdhara adheres to the latter sense.

On vi. 75, 13 (=Vâj. S. xxix. 50), I quote Prof. Wilson's note, from which it will be seen that the interpreters are at variance: "*Prachetasaḥ* is applied by Yâska, ix. 20, and Mahîdhara, to *aṣvân,* the intelligent horses; but Sâyaṇa is better advised, as there is no other nominative to the verbs *janghanti* and *jighnate.*" I think, however, that from the position of *prachetasaḥ* in the verse it is difficult to conect it in the way Sâyaṇa does.

vii. 3, 7. *Pûrbhiḥ* is here rendered "cities," but "protectors" (*pâlakaiḥ*) in vi. 48, 8, where it occurs in a similar connection. It probably means "rampart," as in fact Sâyaṇa himself intimates on vii. 15, 14; *Pûḥ purî tad-rakshâ-sâdhana-bhûta-prâkâr-* (qu. *prâkâr-*) *âdir vâ,* "*Pur* is a city, or walls, etc., which are the means of its defence."

vii. 4, 7. *Parishadyam* is translated either as "fit" (*paryâptam*), or "to be taken away" (*pariharttavyam*); and *araṇa,* here rendered "freedom from debt," is in verse 8 explained as *aramamâṇ* , "not delighting."

vii. 5, 3. *Pûru,* here and in vi. 46, 8, explained as the "name of a king," is in vii. 8, 4, interpreted as the "name of an Asura;[1] and in i. 63, 7, as an epithet of Sudâs, in the sense of, "satisfying with offerings." In iv. 21, 10, where the context is partly the same as in i. 63, 7, *pûru* is explained "man," "sacrificer." In i. 130, 7, after saying that *pûru* signifies "one who fills up, offers, what is desired," Sâyaṇa ends by telling us that the word is one of the names for "man."

ibid. 7. *Vâyur na pâthaḥ paripâsi* is explained as, "thou drinkest soma like Vâyu," or "thou drinkest up, driest, water like Vâyu."[2]

vii. 6, 4. The subject of the participle *madantîḥ* is said to be either "creatures" (*prajâḥ*), or "dawns" (*ushasaḥ*).

vii. 8, 4 (=Vâj. S. xii. 34). *Ṣṛṇve* is rendered by Sâyaṇa, "is renowned," whilst Mahîdhara makes it, "hears the invocation of the worshipper."

ibid. 6. *Dvibarhâḥ* is explained as "great in knowledge and works," or "great in two worlds."

vii. 16, 1 (=Vâj. S. xv. 32). *Arati* is explained by Sâyaṇa as goer" or "lord;" by Mahîdhara as "having competent understanding," or "of ceaseless activity."

ibid. 7 (=Vâj. S. xxxiii. 14.) *Yantâraḥ* is rendered by Sâyaṇa "givers," and by Mahîdhara, "controuling their senses." Sâyaṇa assigns to *sûrâyaḥ* in the same verse the sense of "impellers," or of "praisers."

vii. 18, 6. *Matsyâso niṣitâḥ* is rendered either "like fish confined," or "Matsyas (people so called) harassed;" and *ṣrushṭi*, either "quick arrival," or "happiness," while in *v.* 10 it receives the former sense, and in vii. 40, 1 the latter.

ibid. 8. *Bheda* is explained either "unbeliever" (*nâstika*), or as the name of an enemy of Sudâs (which latter sense is also assigned in vii. 33, 3).

vii. 23, 4 (=Vâj. S. xxxiii. 18), *Âpaṣ chit pipyuḥ staryo na gâvaḥ*: Sâyaṇa: "Let the waters increase like barren

[1] So, too, Mahîdhara on Vâj. S. xii. 34.

[2] Both explanations seem to be wrong. Compare the words *Vishṇurgopâḥ paramam pâti pâthaḥ*, in iii. 55, 10, where Sâyaṇa himself renders the last three words "guards the highest place," though he adds an optional rendering of *pâthaḥ* as the "place of water, the atmosphere."

cows." Mahîdhara: "The waters swell the soma like the Vedic texts, with which libations are offered."

vii. 32, 18 (= S.V. i. 310), compared with viii. 19, 26. In the former passage, the words *na pâpatvâya râsîya*, which are common to both, are explained by *na dadyâm*: "I would not give, *i.e.* I would not give up, my worshipper to wretchedness." (Comp. Müller's transl. of this verse, in his Anc. Sansk. Lit. p. 545. In viii. 1, 22, *râsate* is explained by *dadâti*: "he gives.") In viii. 19, 26, however, the same words, *na râsîya*, though employed in a similar connection, are explained by *na âkroṣayeyam*: "I would not cause thee to be reviled." Prof. Wilson there translates as follows: "May I not be accused, Vasu, of calumniating thee, nor, gracious (Agni), of sinfulness against thee," etc.: instead of which Mr. Cowell proposes to render: "Let me not abuse thee by calumny or wickedness," which is no material improvement. There can be little doubt, I think, that Sâyaṇa, followed by his translators, is wrong, and that the verse should be taken in conjunction with the preceding (v. 25) and (omitting epithets) be explained as follows: "If, Agni, thou wert a mortal, and I an immortal, I should not give thee up to execration, or to wretchedness," etc.[1] We have Sâyaṇa's own authority on vii. 32, 18, as I have shown, for rendering *na râsîya*: "I would not give;" and although he does not explain *pâpatvâya* at all in either of these passages, he does distinctly assign to it the sense of "wretchedness" (*hînabhâvâya*) in a similar text, vii. 94, 3: "Do not, ye heroes, Indra and Agni, subject us to wretchedness (*pâpatvâya*), or to execration, or to reviling." Comp. Benfey's rendering of Sâma-veda, i. 310, and ii. 268.

vii. 41, 2 (=Vâj. S. xxxiv. 35.) *Tura* is rendered by Sâyaṇa "wealthy;" by Mahîdhara "sick," or as a designation of "Yama."

vii. 48, 3. *Uparatâti* is explained here as = *upalatâti*, "that which is carried on with stones, a battle." On i. 151, 5, it is explained as "that which has an extension of clouds."

[1] There are other instances in the hymns of the sense running on from one verse into another. See vv. 5 and 6 of this same hymn, viii. 10, and viii. 12, 32 f. in Prof. Wilson's translation.

vii. 64, 1. The words *ghṛtasya nirṇijaḥ* are interpreted either "forms of water" discharged by the clouds, or "forms of melted butter" offered to Mitra and Varuṇa.

vii. 66, 9. The verb *dhîmahi* is interpreted here, "we hold, or have;" on iii, 62, 10 (the celebrated *gâyatrî*), "we meditate" (*dhyâyâmaḥ*), or "let us hold in our mind as an object of contemplation" (*dheyatayâ manasâ dhârayema*), or "we hold" (*dhârayâmaḥ*). In vii. 15, 7, *nidhîmahî* is explained, "we have placed;" and in i. 17, 6, "we deposit as a treasure."

vii. 71, 4. *Viṣvapsnya* is explained as "pervading" (*vyâptarûpa*), or as a name of Vasishṭha.

vii. 77, 2. *Gavaṃ mâtâ* is said to mean the "former, either of voices, or of cows."

vii. 79, 3. *Angirastamâ*, an epithet of Ushas (the Dawn), is explained as either "the quickest of goers," or as a designation given to her, because night was produced along with the Bharadvâjas of the race of Angiras, and she (the Dawn) forms the end of the night!

vii. 82, 1. *Mahi ṣarma* is explained as either a "great house, or "great happiness."

ibid. 5. *Ṣubham îyate* is explained either, "obtains an ornament," or "sends water."

vii. 83, 2. *Svardṛṣ* is here explained "seeing heaven after quitting the body." In vii. 58, 2, it is interpreted, "seer of the sun, *i.e.* living creature," or "tree, from its seeing the sky."

vii. 90, 1 (=Vâj. S. xxxiii. 70.) *Vîrayâ* is taken by Sâyaṇa for a dative masc. "to the hero (Vâyu);" whilst Mahîdhara joins with it the preceding *pra* and makes *pravîrayâ* an epithet of the soma libations, with the sense, "having excellent heroes sprung from knowledge, priests."

ibid. 3 (=Vaj. S. xxvii. 24.) Sâyaṇa takes *nireke* for "in poverty," and Mahîdhara for "in a place crowded with people."

ibid. 5. *Vîravâham* is explained either to be "borne by worshippers, or by horses."

vii. 99, 3 (=Vaj. S.V. 16.) *Mayûkhaiḥ* is rendered by

Sâyaṇa "mountains,"[1] while Mahîdhara understands it of "various glorious lives (*sva-tejo-rûpair nânâ jîvaiḥ*), or his numerous incarnations in a Boar," etc.

vii. 104, 2. *Ghorachakshas* is explained as either "horrible in aspect," or "harshly speaking."

viii. 1, 2. *Ubhayâvinam* is explained as either "having both celestial and earthly riches," or "having both stationary and moving things to preserve," or "having persons both to praise and sacrifice to him."

ibid. 10. *Gâyatravepas* is explained here "having approved speed," whilst on i. 142, 12, it is interpreted as "having the form of the *gâyatra*."

Ibid. 31. *Yâdvaḥ* is explained as either "of the race of Yadu," or "renowned among men," and *paṣu* as either "having cattle," or "a perceiver of what is minute."

viii. 3, 5. *Samîke* is interpreted as either "at sacrifice," or in battle."

ibid. 9. *Yatibhyaḥ* is explained as either "from non-sacrificing men," or "for men practising rites."

ibid. 24. *Turîya* is explained either "fourth," or a "destroyer of enemies."

viii. 4, 8. *Dâna* is interpreted either a "breaker up," (*avakhaṇḍayitâ*) or a "giver."

viii. 5, 9. *Vi pathaḥ sitam* is explained either "shut up the paths that others may not enter," or the contrary, "open up, show the paths."

ibid. 13. *Brahma janânâm* is interpreted as either "the Brâhman-caste among men," or "the prayer, or the sacrificial food, of men."

ibid. 38. *Charmamnâḥ* is explained as either "practised in the wearing of cuirasses of leather," or "exercised in the use of horses and other instruments of motion." The word is interpreted by Mahîdhara on Vaj. S. xxx. 15, as "a person practised in the handling of leather (*charmâbhyâsa-karam*.")

viii. 6, 3. *Jâmi* is interpreted as either "useless," or "kinsman," *âyudham* as either "weapon," or "assailant," and

[1] Sâyaṇa adds, "For mountains belong to Vishṇu as his own, as the Veda says 'Vishṇu is lord of the mountains.'"

kaṇvâh as either "encomiasts," or "persons of the family of Kaṇva."

viii. 12, 1. *Mada* is explained as either the "exhilaration" of Indra, or "to be exhilarated," or "exhilarated."

viii. 13, 1. The words *kratum ukthyam* are explained either "the performer of the rite and the encomiast," or the "sacrifice called *ukthya*."

ibid. 3. *Bharâya* is explained either "to the battle," or "to the sacrifice," and it is added that the same words generally denote both these things.

viii. 15, 2. The word *ajrân* is taken as an epithet of the preceding term *girîn*, "mountains or clouds," and explained as "quickly moving." It is diversely interpreted in other passages. On viii. 27, 18, it is made to signify the "city of the enemy, although impregnable against the assaults of others," or "level ground;" on iv. 1, 17, "the undecaying, mountains," or "the moving, rays;" on iv. 19, 7, "travelling on the road;" on v. 54, 4, "clouds." I do not know how Sâyaṇa renders it in x. 44, 8, and x. 59, 3. Prof. Roth renders it "*ager*, field," and Prof. Goldstücker, "field, acre, plain," and also as an adjective, "quick." The sense of "plains" is fixed by the context of x. 59, 3, as, at least, one of the right ones: "Let us by our manly deeds overcome our enemy, as the sky (is over) the earth, and the mountains (over) the plains" (*girayo na ajrân*).

viii. 17, 5. *Kukshyoḥ* is interpreted either, in Indra's "two bellies; (as it is written 'fill both bellies, that of the slayer of Vṛttra, and that of Maghavat'") or "the right and left sides, or the upper and lower parts, of a single belly."

Ibid. 12. *Ṣâchigu* is explained as either "he who has strong cows," or "he who has manifest, famous, rays, or cows."

ibid. 13. *Ṣṛngavṛsho napât* is explained as either "the son of *Ṣringavrish*," or *ṣṛngavṛsh* is "the showerer of rays, the sun," and *napât* "he who causes not to fall, who establishes," and therefore the two words together mean "the establisher of the sun."

ibid. 15. *Pṛdâkusânu* is explained as either "having the

head erect like a serpent," or "to be propitiated like a serpent."

viii. 18, 21. *Trivarûtha* is explained as either "affording protection from three inconveniences—cold, heat, and rain," or "having three stories."

The following are some additional instances of the same description, chiefly from the earlier books of the Rig-veda.

i. 31, 2, and i. 112, 4. *Dvimâtâ*, an epithet of Agni, is explained by Sâyana as either "born from two pieces of wood," *i.e.* by friction, and so having two parents, or "maker of the two worlds." Compare *dvijanmâ* in i. 140, 2, and i. 149, 4, which, in the former place, he interprets either "born from two pieces of wood," or by "friction and the subsequent rite of consecration;" while in the second passage a third sense of "born from heaven and earth," is added. In i. 112, 4, the verb *vibhûshati* is rendered either "pervades," or "adorns." So, also, *paribhûshathaḥ* in iii. 12, 9, is declared to mean either "ye are adorned" (*alankṛtau bhavathaḥ*), or, "ye overcome" (*paribhavathaḥ*). See, above, the different senses assigned by Yâska to *paryabhûshat*.

i. 64, 10. *Vṛsha-khâdayaḥ*, an epithet of the Maruts, is explained as either, "having Indra for their weapon," or "having soma for their beverage." The word is rendered "adorned with ear-rings," by Bollensen (in Benfey's Orient und Occident, ii. 461, note), who refers for the meaning he assigns to *vṛsha* to Wilson's Dictionary, *s.v.*, *vṛshabha*, where one of the senses given is, "the orifice of the ear." *Khâdi* occurs frequently in the R.V. in the sense of an ornament worn by the Maruts, as in v. 53, 4; v. 54, 11, where it is rendered by Sâyana *kaṭaka*, and in vii. 56, 13, where he renders it *alankâra-viṣesha*. On i. 168, 3, he makes it mean "a guard to the hand," *hasta-trâṇaka*, and on i. 166, 9, either "eatables" or "ornaments." In the last passage he takes *prapatheshu* either for "resting-places," or "toes." Roth, *s.v.*, conjectures that the proper reading here must be *prapadeshu*.

i. 92, 10. *Ṣvaghnî* is here taken by Sâyaṇa for the feminine of *ṣvăhâ* (*lit.* dog-killer), and is rendered *vyâdha-strî*, a "hunter's wife." The word is, however, explained by Yâska

(Nir. v. 22, where he quotes R.V. x. 43, 5) as = *kitava*, "a gamester." This sense is adopted by Sâyaṇa himself on viii. 45, 38. On ii. 12, 4, dropping all reference to any feminine sense, he explains the word as "hunter" (*vyâdha*), viz., "one who kills wild animals with dogs" (*ṣvabhir mṛgân hanti*); and in the same way on iv. 20, 3, as *mṛgayu*, "a hunter." See Benfey's note on i. 92, 10, in his version of the passage in his Orient und Occident, ii. 257; and Bollensen's translation of the verse in the same vol., p. 464. If Yâska is right in explaining *ṣvaghnî* as a masculine noun, signifying "gamester," it can scarcely be also the feminine of *ṣvahâ*; or if it be the latter, it cannot well have a masculine sense also. I observe, also, that Sâyaṇa renders the word *vijaḥ* "birds" in i. 92, 10; and "one who causes distress" (*udvejaka*) in ii. 12, 5.

i. 128, 4. *Ishûyate* is said to mean either "to him who desires food," or "to him who desires coming."

i. 169, 5. The words *tve râyas toṣatamaḥ* are rendered either "thy riches are most gladdening," or "thy kinsmen, friends (the Maruts), are most destructive (to clouds which do not rain)."

i. 173, 6. *Opaṣa* is here explained as either a "horn," or "earth and atmosphere." On viii. 14, 5, the scholiast makes it either "a cloud lying near" (*megham upetya ṣayânam*), or "some particular manly power contained in himself" (*i.e.* in Indra, *âtmani samaveto vîrya-viṣeshaḥ*.

i. 190, 5. The words *chayase piyârum* are explained by Sâyaṇa as either, "thou visitest, with the view of favouring, him who drinks, offers, soma," or "thou destroyest the destructive man." The latter interpretation is supported by Nir. iv. 25, to which Sâyaṇa refers; and is adopted by him in iii. 30, 8.

ii. 1, 4. *Asura* is explained here as either, "the expeller of foes" (*ṣatrûṇâṃ nirasitâ*), or "the giver of strength, the sun." This word is very variously interpreted by Sâyaṇa in different places. On i. 24, 14, he makes it = *anishṭa-kshepaṇa-ṣîla*, "the hurler away of what is undesired;" on i. 35, 7, *sarveshâṃ prâṇada*, "the giver of life to all;" on i. 54, 3, either, "the expeller of enemies," or "he who has breath, or force," or "the giver of breath, or water;" on i. 64, 2, and i. 174, 1, expellers of enemies;" on i. 108, 6, "thrower of oblations, priest;" on i. 110, 3, an unexplained designation of Tvashtri, perhaps in the later sense of "evil spirit;" on i. 131, 1, "expeller of unrighteous enemies;" on i. 151, 4, "strong;" on ii. 27, 10, *ṣatrûṇâm kshepaka*, "hurler away of enemies; on iv. 2, 5; iv. 53, 1; v. 12, 1; v. 15, 1; v. 27, 1; vii. 2, 3; vii. 6, 1; vii. 30, 3; vii. 36, 2, "strong; on v. 42, 1, "giver of breath;" ibid. *v*. 11, "strong," or "giver of breath;" on v. 51, 11, "expeller of enemies, or giver of breath, or force;" on v. 41, 3, "taker away of breath" (Rudra), or "giver of breath" (Sûrya or Vâyu); on iii. 3, 4 "giver of strength;" on iii. 29, 14, "the impelling" (*araṇi*-wood); on v. 63, 3, 7, "the expeller (or discharger) of water, Parjanya;" on v. 83, 6, the same sense; on vii. 56, 1, "wise" (*prajnâvân*); on viii. 20, 17, "a water-discharging cloud," or "rain water;" on viii. 25, 4, "powerful," or "as pervading all things, impellers;" on viii. 79, 6, "powerful, or possessor of life." In the Nighaṇṭus i. 10, *asura* is given as one of the synonymes of "cloud." In Nir. iii. 8, it is said to be = *asu-rata*, "devoted to breath," or to come from *sthâneshu* or *sthânebhyaḥ asta*, "thrown in, or from, places;" or *asu* is a synonyme of *prâṇa*, "life," a thing "thrown into the body. The Asuras are they who have it." And he adds, "it is well known that he (the creator) formed the *Suras* (gods) from *su*, "good," in which their essence consists, and that he formed the Asuras from *asu* (or *a* + *su*, "not good"), and that in this consists their essence." It is to be observed that the verse here explained by Yâska (R.V. x. 53, 4) is one of those later texts in which the word *asura* has the sense of evil spirit, as an enemy of the gods, a sense which it does not generally bear in the older hymns, in which it is a designation of the gods themselves. (In vii. 13, 1, however, Agni is called an "Asura-slayer," as is also Indra in vii. 22, 4).

ii. 11, 21. *Mâ ati dhak* is explained by Sâyaṇa either "do not give to others, passing us by," or "do not burn up our objects of desire."

vi. 2, 7. *Trayâyya* is explained by Sâyaṇa as either, "to be preserved," or "one who has the three qualifications of science, austerity and works," or "one who has attained to the three births."[1]

viii. 24, 24. *Paripadâm* is explained by Sâyaṇa as either "persons who are sacrificing around," or "birds which are flying around."

Ṣvâtra is given in Nigh. ii. 10, among the synonymes of *dhana*, "wealth." In Nir. v. 3, it is said to mean "quick" (*ṣvâtram iti kshipra-nâma âṣu atanaṃ bhavati*); and the words of R.V. x. 88, 4, *sa patatrîtvaraṃ sthâ jagad yach chhvâtram Agnir akṛṇoj jâtavedâḥ* are explained: "Agni Jâtavedas made *quickly* whatever flies, goes, stands or moves." The term is also found in R.V. i. 31, 4, where the clause *ṣvâtreṇa yat pitror muchyase pari*, spoken of Agni, is rendered by Sâyaṇa: "When thou art released from thy parents (the two pieces of wood) by *rapid friction* (*ṣvâtreṇa*)," etc. In viii. 4, 9 (= S.V. i. 277), the word is found in the compound *ṣvâtrabhâj*, an epithet of *vayas* (there stated to mean "food"), and is declared to signify "associated with wealth." In viii. 52, 5, it occurs again in the phrase *ṣvâtram arkâ anûshata*, which the Scholiast interprets, "the worshippers praise *very quickly, very long.*" I am ignorant how he explains the word in x. 46, 7, where it occurs in the plural as an epithet of "fires;" but Mahîdhara on Vâj. S. xxxiii. 1 (where the verse is repeated), assigns to it the sense of *kshipra-phalaprada*, "quickly bestowing rewards." In Vâj. S. iv. 12, and vi. 34, *ṣvâtra* is found as an epithet of *âpaḥ*, "waters," and in the former of these verses (where "waters" are said to stand for milk) it is explained "quickly digested" (*kshipra-pariṇâmâḥ ṣîghraṃ jîrṇâḥ*), whilst in the second the sense of "quickly effecting the desired object," or "auspicious" (*kshipra-kârya-kâriṇyaḥ ṣivâ vâ*), is assigned. In Vâj. S. v. 31, *ṣvâtra* is used in a sacrificial formula as an epithet of a particular sort of little altar called *Maitravaruṇa-dhishṇya*, and is explained as signifying "friendly" (*mitraḥ*). *Ṣvâtrya* appears to be an epithet of Soma in R.V. x. 49, 10,

[1] In *v.* 11 of this hymn Sâyaṇa explains the pronoun *tâ*, "these," as meaning the "sins committed in another birth,"—a further instance of his ascribing more modern notions to the Vedic age.

as it is of *girah*, "hymns," in x. 160, 2; but I am not aware how it is explained in those passages by the Commentator. On the whole, looking to the variety of senses ascribed to the word *ṣvâtra*, and to the artificial processes by which those senses are sometimes reached, I cannot but think that the Scholiasts were not always sure of its real signification.

I have, perhaps, already adduced a superabundance of instances in which Sâyaṇa, or Yâska, gives double, and, therefore, uncertain, interpretations of obscure words in the Rig-veda. But if any reader desires to pursue the subject further, he may examine for himself the following additional illustrations of the same fact which are indicated in the notes to the first three volumes of Prof. Wilson's translation of the Rig-veda, and have been verified by a reference to the Commentary of Sâyaṇa:—

R.V. i. 43, 4; i. 50, 4; i. 51, 4; i. 62, 4; i. 65, 3; i. 68, 1; i. 84, 16, 18; i. 89, 6; i. 95, 6; i. 97, 1; i. 100, 14; i. 102, 9; i. 105, 1, 8; i. 110, 6; i. 115, 1; i. 122, 2, 14; i. 123, 3; i. 124, 7; i. 125, 7; i. 127, 7; i. 129, 10; i. 130, 9; i. 132, 3; i. 141, 3; i. 143, 3; i. 145, 4; i. 146, 1; i. 149, 4; i. 150, 1 (comp. Nir. v. 11); i. 150, 3; i. 151, 2; i. 152, 1; i. 154, 4; i. 155, 2; i. 156, 4; i. 157, 2, 4; i. 164 (*passim*); i. 165, 5, 15; i. 169, 4, 6; i. 173, 2; i. 174, 7; i. 175, 4; i. 178, 2; i. 180, 7; i. 181, 3, 6; i. 182, 1, 2; i. 188, 5; i. 191, 8; ii. 2, 5; ii. 6, 2 (comp. viii. 50, 7); ii. 11, 3; ii. 12, 8; ii. 13, 11; ii. 18, 8; ii. 19, 4; ii. 20, 7; ii. 23, 17; ii. 24, 10; ii. 27, 8, 15; ii. 34, 2; ii. 38, 10; iii. 15, 1, 2; iii. 17, 1, 3; iii. 51, 3; iii. 60, 6; iii. 61, 2 (compared with i. 113, 12); iii. 61, 5; iv. 1, 5, 16; iv. 2, 1, 11; iv. 3, 7; iv. 9, 4; iv. 42, 1, 4, 8; iv. 44, 2; iv. 50, 6; iv. 53, 1; iv. 55, 1; iv. 56, 6; iv. 58, 1 and *passim*; v. 1, 6, 8; v. 7, 3; v. 8, 2; v. 9, 4; v. 33, 1; v. 36, 3; v. 50, 3; v. 69, 1; v. 73, 5; v. 74, 1, 8, 10; v. 75, 9; v. 76, 1; v. 79, 5; v. 86, 1; v. 87, 1; vi. 1, 4; vi. 4, 7; vi. 15, 3; vi. 17, 7; vi. 18, 14; vi. 26, 4;[1] vi. 26, 6; vi. 29, 2; vi. 34, 4;

[1] Sâyaṇa here refers, in illustration of one of his views, to another passage, x. 49, 4.

vi. 35, 5; vi. 44, 7; vi. 49, 7, 14; vi. 51, 6; vi. 56, 3; vi. 59, 6; vi. 61, 3.

In addition to these numerous instances, in which Sayaṇa proposes double interpretations, Prof. Wilson points out in his notes frequent differences of opinion between Sâyaṇa and Mahîdhara in regard to the rendering of passages which are common to the Rig-veda and the Vâjasaneyi Sanhitâ.

I will add some specimens of what appear to me to be mistranslations on the part of Sâyaṇa.

R.V. i. 22, 20 (=Vâj. S. vi. 5) he explains thus: "The wise ever behold with scriptural gaze (*ṣâstra-dṛshṭyâ*) that supreme station of Vishṇu, as the eye extended on every side in the sky, clear from the absence of any obstacle, beholds." He thus makes *chakshus*, "the eye," a nominative, and supplies *paṣyati*, "beholds." Mahîdhara, however, taking *chakshus* as an accusative, renders, as it appears to me, correctly, "like an eye extended in the clear sky," or (dropping the particle denoting resemblance) "that eye, the orb of the sun, which is extended in the sky;" and he quotes Vâj. S. vii. 42 (=R.V. i. 115, 1) and xxxvi. 24 (=R.V. vii. 66, 16) to show that the orb of the sun (represented here by Vishṇu) is called an "eye." Compare also R.V. vi. 51, 1; vii. 61, 1; vii. 63, 1; vii. 76, 1; x. 37, 1. "The wise" thus, according to Mahîdhara, "behold the highest station of Vishṇu fixed in the sky, like an eye." This construction is also adopted by Benfey in his version of the hymn.

i. 25, 11, is rendered by Wilson, following Sâyaṇa, "through him (*ataḥ* = *asmâd Varuṇât*), the sage (*chikitvân*) beholds," etc.; but better by Müller (Anc. Sansk. Lit. p. 536), "from thence perceiving (*chikitvân*)," etc., "he (Varuṇa) sees," etc. Similarly Benfey.

ibid. v. 13. The words *pari spaṣo nishedire* are explained by Sâyaṇa: "the gold-touching rays were diffused (*nishaṇṇâh*, placed) on every side." Müller renders better: "the spies sat down around him." So, too, Benfey. Compare A.V. iv. 16, 4, where there can be no doubt that the word *spaṣah* means "messengers" or "spies." See also the remarks which I have made above on this term.

i. 91, 3. The first words of this verse are rendered by Wilson, "thy acts are (like those) of the royal Varuṇa," in conformity with the second of the two interpretations proposed by Sâyaṇa. The first, which Wilson rejects, is as follows: "*Varuṇa* is soma bought for sacrifice and covered with a cloth (*vastreṇâvṛtaḥ*): all the ceremonies, the *agnishṭhoma*, etc., are connected with thee when purchased; hence thou art the instrument in all sacrifices."

vii. 32, 18 (on which, as well as on the passage to be next quoted, viii. 19, 25 f., I have already made some remarks), is rendered as follows by Professor Müller (Anc. Sansk. Lit. p. 545:) "If I were lord of as much as thou, I should support the sacred bard, thou scatterer of wealth, I should not abandon him to misery. 19. I should award wealth day by day to him who magnifies; I should award it to whosoever it be. We have no other friend but thee," etc. But Sâyaṇa understands the first clause of *v.* 19, not as a continuation of the words of the worshipper, as it appears to be, but as spoken by Indra: "Having heard these words of Indra," he says, "the rishi, delighted, exclaims, 'we have no other friend,'" etc. This appears to be wrong.

viii. 19, 25 f. is a passage closely resembling the preceding. It begins thus: *Yad Agne martyas tvaṃ syâm aham mitramaho amartyaḥ*, and should, I think, be translated as follows: "If, Agni, thou (wert) a mortal, (and) were I, o amicably-shining[1] god, an immortal, o invoked son of strength,—(26) I would not abandon thee to malediction, or to poverty; my worshipper should not be poor or distressed," etc. Verse 25 would thus form the protasis and verse 26 the apodosis. But Sâyana takes the 25th verse by itself and explains it thus: "If I, a mortal, were thou, *i.e.* if I should, by worshipping thee, acquire thy nature, then I should become an immortal, a god." My interpretation is borne out by a parallel passage (which is not, like the preceding, elliptical in construction), viii. 44, 23. *Yad Agne syâm ahaṃ tvaṃ tvaṃ vâ gha syâ aham | syus te satyâ ihâśishaḥ*, which Sâyaṇa renders, "If I were thou,

[1] I adopt here Sâyaṇa's rendering of *mitramahas*, whether it be correct or not.

(wealthy), or thou wert I (a poor worshipper), then thy wishes would be fulfilled." Compare also viii. 14, 1, 2.

It is true R.V. i. 38, 4, 5, may be quoted on the other side. The original of this passage is as follows: 4. *Yad yûyaṃ pṛṣnimâtaraḥ martâsaḥ syâtana* | *stotâ vo amṛtaḥ syât.* | 5. *Mâ vo mṛgo na yavase jaritâ bhûd ajoshyaḥ* | *pathâ yamasya gâd upa* | which Sâyaṇa renders: "Although you, sons of Priṣni, were mortals, yet your worshipper would be immortal, a god. (Prof. Wilson's version of this verse does not correctly represent Sâyaṇa). 5. Let not your panegyrist be an object of disregard (as a wild animal is not regardless of grass in a pasture), or go along the path of Yama." Rosen renders: "4. Licet vos, Prisnis filii! mortales fueritis, *tamen* laudator vester immortalis esse poterit. 5. Nunquam vester laudator, cervi instar in prato, sit negligendus, *neque* Yamæ viam calcet." Benfey translates: "4. If you, o children of Priṣni, were mortals, an immortal would then be your panegyrist. 5. Let not him who praises you be an object of indifference to you, like a wild animal at grass; let him not walk along the path of Yama." And he gives the following paraphrase of *v.* 4: "Ye are so great, that if ye were men, the gods would sing your praises." Professor Aufrecht would render: "Even if ye were mortals (and not gods, as you are in reality), it would require an immortal to praise you (worthily)." I cannot say that these interpretations appear to me particularly satisfactory. If we could suppose an aposiopesis at the end of *v.* 4, the sense might be: "If ye were mortals, and your worshipper an immortal, *i.e.* if you and I were to change places, I would not be so careless about my worshippers as you are about yours." Or can we suppose that the Rishi is expressing an aspiration that he could change places with the objects of his adoration? Or, possibly, the meaning might be: "If ye were mortal [*i.e.* if ye knew by experience the sufferings of mortality], your worshipper should be [ye would make him] immortal." This perhaps derives some confirmation from the deprecation of death in the next verse.

vii. 89, 1, is thus explained by Sâyaṇa: "Let me not go, o

king Varuṇa, to thy earthen house; but may I attain to thy resplendent golden house." The sense seems simply to be what Müller makes it: "Let me not yet, o Varuṇa, enter into the house of clay," *i.e.* the grave. Compare A.V. v. 30, 14, *mâ nu gâd mâ nu bhûmigṛho bhuvat,* "let him not go; let him not have the earth for his house."

x. 160, 4, is also, as it appears to me, incorrectly rendered by Sâyaṇa. His explanation, as translated by Prof. Goldstücker, in his Dictionary, *s.v. aratni,* is as follows: "Indra manifests himself (to the pious); (the sacrificer), who, though not wealthy, offers him the soma libation,—him, Indra, the wealthy, holds in his hand (lit. *fist*, *i.e.* he protects him), after having defeated his enemies," etc. I would propose the following as a correcter translation: "That man is observed by him (Indra) who, being rich, pours out to him no soma libation," etc. See my former paper "On the relations of the priests to the other classes of Indian Society," p. 293, note 2, where this translation is vindicated.

Some instances have already been given, in which Sâyaṇa imports the ideas of a later age into his interpretation of the hymns. I give a few more illustrations of this tendency, both as it regards mythological and speculative conceptions.

In i. 170, 2, it is said: "Why dost thou seek to kill us, Indra? the Maruts are thy brothers." On this the Commentator remarks: "The Maruts are Indra's brothers, from having been produced from the same womb of Aditi; and this production is celebrated in the Purâṇas." On this Professor Wilson annotates: "Here, probably, nothing more is meant than affinity of function." The Maruts are not Âdityas according to the Rig-veda, and even Indra himself is not generally so called in the hymns. See my Art. on "Vedic Cosmogony," etc., p. 39. In iii. 53, 5, the worshippers address Indra as "brother."

In vii. 72, 2, the Aṣvins are thus addressed: "For there are paternal friendships between us, a common bond,—acknowledge it." On this Sâyaṇa annotates: "Vivasvat and Varuṇa were both sprung from Kaṣyapa and Aditi. Vivasvat was the father of the Aṣvins (see my Art. on the Aṣvins, in "Contributions to a knowledge of Vedic Theogony," etc., No. ii. p. 2), and Varuṇa of Vasishṭha;" and then he quotes the Brihaddevatâ to prove the second of these relationships, which is also alluded to in R.V. x. 17, 2. The third is perhaps deducible from R.V. vii. 33, 10, ff.; see Sanskrit Texts, i. 75, ff., and Prof. Wilson's translation of the passage. It may be doubtful whether either of those other texts of the R.V. is so old as the one before us. Prof. Roth thinks the verses of R.V. vii. 33, in which Vasishṭha's birth is alluded to, are conceived very much in the taste of the epic mythology, and are attached to an older hymn. But even if both these Vedic legends about the birth of the Aṣvins and Vasishṭha, respectively, are as ancient as the verse I have quoted, vii. 72, 2, still the link by which Sâyaṇa connects them, and which is necessary to establish the relationship of the author of the hymn (supposing him to be Vasishṭha, or a descendant of Vasishṭha) with the Aṣvins, is certainly not Vedic, as we are nowhere told in the hymns that Vivasvat and Varuṇa were sons of Kaṣyapa and Aditi. If Vivasvat be identified with Sûrya, he would, indeed, be, according to some parts of the R.V., an Âditya, or son of Aditi, but not otherwise. See Art. on Vedic cosmogony, p. 75, f. In a later work, the Taittirîya Âraṇyaka i. 13, 3, he is named among the Âdityas. There is no difficulty in supposing that the passage before us does not contain any mythological allusion. In other places also reference is made to the former (vi. 18, 5) or ancestral (vi. 21, 8; i. 71, 10) friendship of the worshippers with the gods.

In i. 114, 6, Rudra is called the father of the Maruts. To explain this Sâyaṇa *in loco* tells a story that: "Indra, once on a time, overcame the Asuras, when Diti, their mother, desiring to have a son who should be able to avenge her vanquished sons by slaying the Thunderer, practised austerity and became pregnant by her husband. Indra, learning this news, entered into her womb in a very minute form, with a thunderbolt in his hand, divided her fœtus into seven parts, and again made each of those parts into seven. These fragments all issued from the womb and wept. At this conjuncture Paramesvara (Rudra), and Pârvatî (his wife), were passing by for amusement, and saw them. Pârvatî said to her husband: 'If you love me, make all these bits of flesh become severally sons.' He accordingly made them all of the same form and age, and decked with similar ornaments, and gave them to her, saying: 'Let them be thy sons.'" The Maruts ought thus to be ($7 \times 7 = 49$) forty-nine in number. In R.V. viii. 28, 5, however, (if, indeed, the Maruts are there intended) they are only spoken of as seven. Sâyaṇa there gives a modified version of the story, to the effect that when Aditi (not Diti) desired to have a son equal to Indra, and her fœtus had, from some cause, been split into seven by Indra, the seven parts became seven troops (of Maruts).

It may be questioned whether, in styling Varuna, in conformity with modern ideas, "the deity presiding over the waters" (*jalâbhimânî devaḥ*), (as he does in R.V. i. 161, 14; viii. 58, 12), Sâyana does not derive some support from expressions in the hymns themselves. (See the passages quoted in pp. 86 f. of my "Contributions to a Knowledge of Vedic Theogony," etc.) In one of those texts, however, vii. 49, 3, the waters, in the midst of which Varuna is said to move, "beholding the truth and falsehood of men," seem to be rather aerial than oceanic, as the former, from their position above the earth, would appear to afford to the god (when anthropomorphically regarded) a more convenient post of observation than the latter. And in vii. 64,2, the epithet, *sindhupatî*, "lords of the sea," (or "of rivers," *nadyâḥ pâlayitârau*, Sâyaṇa), is applied not only to Varuṇa but to Mitra also, who is not, that I am aware of, ever connected with the sea, even in later mythology. If we add to this, that these two gods are solicited to send *food and rain from the sky*, it may result that they are called *sindhupatî*, as supplying the aerial waters by which terrestrial streams are filled. But Sâyaṇa does not generally style Varuṇa the god of the sea, but in conformity with older conceptions, the deity who presides over the night. (See the paper above quoted, pp. 77 f.)

The epithet *Kauşika* is applied in R.V. i. 10, 11, to Indra

Sâyaṇa says it means son of Kuṣika, and repeats a story from the Anukramaṇikâ, or Index to the R.V., which relates that that person, wishing a son like Indra, practised chastity, in consequence of which Indra was born to him in the form of Gâthin. Roth, *s.v.* thinks the epithet may have originally meant "belonging, devoted to the Kuṣikas." The word is given in the Amara Kosha as denoting Indra, bdellium, owl, and snakecatcher.

I have mentioned above that Sâyaṇa understands R.V. i. 22, 16, 17, to refer to one of the incarnations of Vishṇu. On *v.* 16, he speaks of Vishṇu as *parameṣvara*, "the supreme deity." On i. 156, 4, he proposes either to take Vishṇu for the sacrifice, according to the idea of the Brâhmaṇas, or as the creator (*vedhas*) of the Maruts, whose function as preserver Varuṇa and the other gods recognize.

On i. 43, 1, Sâyaṇa derives the name Rudra from the root *rud*, "to weep," denoting the god who "makes everything to weep at the time of the end," and thus identifies him with the Mahâdeva of later mythology. (See Wilson's note *in loco*).

Sâyaṇa gives, optionally, a spiritual meaning to the words in i. 50, 10: "looking aloft to the upper light above the darkness, the Sun, a god among the gods, we have arrived at the highest luminary." He says the phrase "above the darkness" may mean "above the night," or "above sin;" and quotes a text which explains this passage and declares that "darkness is sin," etc.

On R.V. i. 71, 4, Prof. Wilson's note will further illustrate Sâyaṇa's practice of introducing later ideas into his explanations: "Mâtariṣvan is a common name of Vâyu, or wind; but it is here said to mean the principal vital air (*mukhya-prâṇa*) divided (*vibhṛta*) into the five airs so denominated, as in a dialogue between them, cited by the Scholiast, etc., etc."[1]

[1] Prof. Wilson has the following remarks in a note on R.V. v. 2, 1: "According to what is no doubt the most accurate interpretation of this verse, and of those which follow, they contain only a metaphorically obscure allusion to the lighting of the sacrificial fire: the mother is the two pieces of touchwood, which retain fire, the child, and will not spontaneously give it up to the father, the *yajamâna*, until

R.V. i. 115, 1 ("The sun, soul of whatever is moving or stationary, has filled heaven, air, and earth") is thus explained by Sâyaṇa: "The sun, existing within such an orb, being, from his pervasiveness, the supreme spirit (*paramâtmâ*), the mover of the universe, is the soul, the substance (*svarûpa-bhûtaḥ*) of whatever is moving or stationary. For he is the cause of all effects stationary or moving; and the effect is not distinct from the cause," etc. "Or, he is the life-soul (*jîvâtmâ*) of all creatures stationary or moving; for when the sun rises, all the world which was before nearly dead, is perceived to be again sentient." Though the latter explanation, no doubt, most nearly approaches the true one, still the first is also proposed by Sâyaṇa as admissible, at least, if not preferable.

Sâyaṇa translates *vedhasaḥ ṣasvataḥ* in i. 72, 1, by *nityasya vidhâtur Brahmaṇaḥ* "of the eternal creator Brahmâ." Though this sense of "eternal creator" is adopted by Benfey, in his version (Or. und Occ. i. p. 601), I should hesitate to admit that it can correctly represent the sense of the ancient bard.

The word *brahmâ* in R.V. i. 164, 35, is explained by Sâyaṇa as *Prajâpati*, though there does not appear to be any reason for supposing that it has that sense anywhere in the R.V., and though the other three clauses of the verse, which relate to sacrifice and objects connected therewith, the altar and the soma-juice, lead to the conclusion that "priest" is the proper rendering.

R.V. iii. 53, 9, is another passage in which Sâyaṇa's interpretation seems to have been influenced by post-vedic legends. We are told in the Râmâyaṇa (i. 60, 2 ff.; see Sanskrit Texts, i. 103), that Viṣvâmitra on a certain occasion created new constellations. Sâyaṇa appears to find a reference to this story in the words *mahân ṛshir devajâ devajûtaḥ*, "the great Rishi, god-born, god-impelled," which

forced by attrition: till then, also, people, the priests, do not behold it, but they see it when bursting into ignition: this, however, has not satisfied the commentators, and a curious and strange legend has been devised for the interpretation of the text, or has been, perhaps, applied to it by way of explanation, having been previously current: it is more probably, however, suggested by, than suggestive of, the verses," etc., etc.

refer to this personage, and which he explains: "The great Rishi, seer of objects beyond the reach of the senses, who had by austerity acquired intense power, generator of shining lights (*devajâ dyotamânânâm tejasâm janayitâ*), drawn by those lights" (*devajûtas tais tejobhir âkṛshṭaḥ*), etc. The real sense of the terms *devajâ devajûtaḥ* seems to be that which I have given above. *Jâḥ* is found in the Nighaṇṭus, ii. 2, as one of the synonymes of *apatya*, "offspring;" and *devajûta* is explained by Sâyaṇa in R.V. vii. 25, 5; viii. 31, 3, as "impelled by the gods" (*devaiḥ prerita*). [It is to be observed, however, that Yâska (x. 28) gives a double interpretation of this latter word, as meaning (in R.V. x. 178, 1) either *deva-gatam deva-prîtam vâ*, "gone to the gods," or "beloved by the gods."] Prof. Wilson partly follows, and partly deviates from, Sâyaṇa, in his translation of R.V. iii. 53, 9, which runs thus: "The great Rishi, the generator of the gods, the attracted by the deities," etc.; and observes, in a note: "*Devajâḥ* is explained by Sâyaṇa, the generator of radiances or energies . . . . . the compound is not *devajâ*, god-born, nor was Viṣvâmitra of divine parentage." In reference to this last remark see Wilson's note on R.V. i. 10, 11, and Sanskrit Texts, i. 82. The non-existence of any Puranic legend ascribing a divine origin to Viṣvâmitra ought not, however, to influence our translation of a Vedic text. And it is not undeserving of notice that, following Sâyaṇa, Prof. Wilson had but shortly before translated R.V. iii. 29, 15, thus: "The Kuṣikas, the first-born of Brahmâ," etc. etc. The Kuṣikas were the tribe to which Viṣvâmitra belonged. Sâyaṇa's words in explanation of this last text are these: *Brahmaṇaḥ sarvasya jagataḥ srashṭuḥ prathamajâḥ prathamotpannaḥ*, "the Kuṣikas, the first-born of Brahmâ, the creator of the whole world." This translation is, however, the result of modern ideas, as I believe it is generally recognized (as already intimated) that there is no passage in the R.V. in which the personal creator (Brahman in the masculine) is mentioned, and in the present case the accent shows that the word is neuter, and therefore signifies "prayer." See the story about the birth of Vasishṭha in R.V. vii. 33, 10 ff. (Sanskrit Texts, i. 75 ff.), and compare the word *devaputra* applied to the Rishis in x. 62, 4, where, though the traditional accent makes the word a *Bahuvrîhi* compound, with the sense, "having gods for their sons," Prof. Roth, *s.v.*, thinks that, with a different accentuation, changing it into a *Tatpurusha*, the meaning may be conjectured to be, "sons of the gods." But if other Rishis were sons of the gods, why should not Viṣvâmitra also have been fabled to be so?

In R.V. iii. 62, 10, (the celebrated Gâyatrî), Savitri is interpreted "the supreme lord, the creator of the world, who impels by his all-pervading presence;" and *bhargas* is "the self-resplendent light, the glory of the supreme Brahma." Another explanation of Savitri as the sun is however given.

The word *tredhâ* in the last clause of R.V. vi. 69, 8, *tredhâ sahaṣram vi tad airayetham* ("ye then scattered a thousand into three parts"), is explained by Sâyaṇa as meaning "existing in the threefold form of world, veda, and speech;" and a Brâhmaṇa is quoted to support the interpretation. (See the entire passage in "Sanskrit Texts," iv. 72, note 42).

In vii. 59, 12. *Tryambaka* is explained as "the father of the three gods, Brahmâ, Vishṇu, and Rudra." This conception of a triad, consisting of these three gods, seems, however, to have been unknown in the Vedic age. Yâska mentions a triad, but it consists of Agni, Vâyu (or Indra), and Sûrya. (See "Sanskrit Texts," iv, 136 f.) I should observe that the passage of Sâyaṇa's Commentary from which this explanation is taken is put by the Editor, Prof. Müller, in brackets, as being derived from only one MS. See the extracts given from the other MSS. in p. 14 of the "Varietas Lectionis" prefixed to the 4th vol. of Müller's R.V. But even if the passage is not genuine, the style of interpretation found in it is that of the modern Indian commentators generally. Mahîdhara explains *tryambaka* as the "three-eyed Rudra." Prof. Wilson holds this text of the Veda to be spurious. The Ṣatapatha Brâhmaṇa, ii. 6, 2, 9, gives another sense of the word *tryambaka*: "He (Rudra) has a sister called Ambikâ, with whom he has this portion: and since he has this portion along with a female (*striyâ saha*), he is called Tryambaka," (*i.e.* Stryambaka). This passage of the Brâhmaṇa refers to Vâj. S. iii. 57, where it is said: "This is thy portion, Rudra, with thy sister Ambikâ."

In vii. 100, 4, it is said that "Vishṇu strode over this earth to give it for an abode to man (or Manu)." Sâyaṇa explains this last word, "to the host of gods who praised him," to whom he was about to give it, "after taking it from the Asuras." This explanation is, apparently, in conformity with more modern legends.

vii. 101, 1. The first clause of this verse, viz., "utter the three words of which light is the first," are explained by Sâyaṇa as meaning "the threefold praises in the form of rich, yajush, and sâman verses, preceded by the brilliant *praṇava*" (or sacred monosyllable Om). An alternative explanation is, however, given, according to which the three words or sounds are "the rapid, the slow, and the intermediate (thunderings), preceded by lightning."

viii. 12, 27. The first words of the verse, addressed to Indra, (which, translated literally, run thus: "when of thee Vishṇu, by the strength," and mean apparently, "when by thy strength Vishṇu strode," etc.), are rendered by Sâyaṇa, "when thy younger brother Vishṇu," etc. Prof. Wilson also observes that they might be translated "when Vishṇu by thy strength." The words "younger brother," *tavânujaḥ*, are not in the original. This idea of Vishṇu being the younger brother of Indra is, I believe, unknown to the Veda, and of modern origin.

In viii. 19, 5, we have the words, "the mortal who worships Agni with fuel, with an oblation, and with *veda*" (whatever that may mean), etc. etc. Sâyaṇa understands it of "reading the Veda," which can scarcely be the sense. See on the meaning of the verse Prof. Müller's "Anc. Sansk. Lit." p. 204 f., referred to by Prof. Wilson *in loco*.

Notwithstanding these instances (which might, no doubt, be considerably multiplied) of Sâyaṇa's tendency to allow the ideas of his own time to influence his exposition of the Veda, I think it must, in fairness, be admitted that, however incapable he may have been of fully comprehending and reproducing the real spirit and genius of the hymns, he introduces into his interpretation of them, on the whole, much less of positive modern mythology and speculation than might, in a writer of his age, have been expected. A similar remark may be made in reference to Yâska, that although in his general observations, Nir. vii. 4, ff., he regards all the deities as being, ultimately, members of the one Soul, he does not, in the sequel, allow this dogmatical view to interfere with his detailed explanations of their individual characteristics.

I extract from the notes to the fourth vol. of Prof. Wilson's translation of the R.V. a few admissions, in his own words, that he, too, occasionally failed to find in Sâyaṇa a perfectly satisfactory guide.

p. 6. "*Gâvaḥ* is rendered by Sâyaṇa *raşmayaḥ*, "rays:" one of its meanings it is true, but rather incompatible here with the verb *vahanti, vehunt*." [1]

p. 94. "The addition of the comment, *devânâm*, seems somewhat superfluous; human wives would have been more in keeping with the prayer." [2]

p. 102. ". . . . . the explanation is not very clear."

p. 103. verse 4. Prof. Wilson departs here, perhaps inadvertently, and I believe wrongly, from Sâyaṇa in rendering *savam*, "birth." The word is explained by Sâyaṇa as = *prasavam, anujnâm*, "permission," but it is rather "impulse." (See my "Contributions to Vedic Theogony," etc., pp. 118 ff.)[3]

p. 144. . . . "he (Sâyaṇa) seems rather puzzled."

p. 179. In his translation of a part of vii. 88, 6, Prof. Wilson deviates from Sâyaṇa's rendering, as he understands it: "*Mâ te enasvanto bhujema*, 'let us not, offending thee, enjoy'—it is not said what: the scholiast attaches the prohibitive to the verb, but gives a different turn to the sentence:

[1] *Atanavat* does not mean "not spreading or dispersing" as Prof. Wilson translates it in p. 28, note 3, but "going," *atana-vat* (not *a-tana-vat*).

[2] Prof. Wilson proposes, in p. 92, to take *ayâtuḥ* as the genitive of *ayâtṛ*, but I know of no such word as the latter with the sense of "one not sacrificing."

[3] In p. 114, Prof. Wilson proposes a translation of a word left unexplained by Sâyaṇa, *svapivâta*, which is founded on an analysis not sanctioned by the Pada-text, as the latter divides the compound *su* + *apivâta*, whilst Wilson would divide it *svapi* + *vâta*.

'being freed from sin through thy favour, let us enjoy enjoyments.'"[1]

p. 211. "The scholiast is rather puzzled how to interpret the duality here intimated."

p. 254. "The second part of the stanza is rendered intelligible by the scholiast only by taking great liberty with some of the terms; and after all the meaning is questionable," etc.

p. 285. *Ṣâchigo* is not very satisfactorily explained," etc.

p. 286. "The construction is loose, and the explanation is not very satisfactory."

To these admissions of Prof. Wilson, taken from the notes to vol. iv., I may add an observation from vol. i. p. 10, on Sâyaṇa's attempts to explain the word *ehimâyâsâḥ*: "It is more than probable that the origin and import of the term were forgotten when Sâyaṇa wrote." But if such was the case in this instance, why not also in many others, in which Sâyaṇa appears to have had no other guide than a fanciful etymology?

The following are some additional instances from the notes to the first, second and third volumes of Prof. Wilson's translation:—

vol. i. p. 211, note. "In this stanza, as usual in the more elaborate metres, we encounter strained collocations and elliptical and obscure illusions, imperfectly transformed into something intelligible by the additions of the scholiast," etc.

p. 215. "This . . . is rather obscure . . . Sâyaṇa does not make it more intelligible," etc.

p. 279. "The terms thus rendered, in conformity to the explanations of the scholiast would seem rather to be intended for proper names," etc. etc. . . . "The meanings may be supported by the etymology of the words, but the interpretation seems to be a needless refinement."

vol. ii. p. 5. "It would make better sense to render it," etc.

p. 36. "The scholiast is evidently puzzled by the phrase."

p. 82. "The scholiast repeats the *Pauranik* legend of the

[1] In a note to p. 193, Mr. Cowell corrects part of Prof. Wilson's translation of vii. 97, 6; but I do not see that the verse contains any word which can be rendered "friendship."

birth of Dîrghatamas from Mamatâ, ... but there is nothing in the text to warrant the application: the persons are obviously allegorical," etc. etc. (Whether Prof. Wilson is right here or not I need not try to decide).

p. 94. "Some of these notions of the commentator are rather *Paurânik* than *Vaidik*."

p. 183. "The passage is not very clear, and Sâyaṇa's explanation does not remove the difficulty."

p. 293. "But this is more of a *Paurânik* than a *Vaidik* legend."

p. 300. "But this is *Paurânik*; apparently not *Vaidik*."

vol. iii. p. 44. "But this is a *Paurânik* notion, Vṛttra, according to the Purânas, being a Brâhman, and by killing him Indra was guilty of the heinous sin of *Brahmahatyâ*."

p. 155. "These explanations are rather, perhaps, derived from the *Paurânik* developments of the original legends, imperfectly handed down."

p. 173. "But this seems to be the notion of a later day."

p. 228. (R.V. v. 31, 7). Prof. Wilson does not follow Sâyaṇa in rendering *mâyâḥ*, "young women," but adheres to the usual sense "devices."

Prof. Wilson also in another place notices the gradual modification of the Vedic ideas by later Indian writers, vol. ii. p. 87: "The Muṇḍaka Upanishad is also quoted for the attainment of heaven, *dyuloka-prâptiḥ*; the figurative expression of the text (R.V. i. 150, 3) having been converted into the assertion of a fact by the Upanishads; instancing the advance from simple metaphor to complex mythological notions."

In the translation of a part of R.V. vi. 59, 1, Prof. Wilson departs from Sâyaṇa. He renders the words *hatâso vâṃ pitaro devaṣatravaḥ* by "the Pitris, the enemies of the gods, have been slain by you, and you survive;" whilst in his note he says: "By Pitris, in this place, the scholiast says Asuras are intended, as derived from the root *pî* to inquire, *pîyatir hiṃsâ-karmâ*."

[The passage is a curious one. The proper translation seems to be: "Your fathers, to whom the gods were hostile, have been slain, whilst you, Indra and Agni, survive."

Professor Aufrecht suggests to me, that a former dynasty of gods is here alluded to as having been destroyed; and he refers, in illustration of this, to R.V. iv. 18, 12: "Who (o Indra) made thy mother a widow? Who sought to kill thee lying or moving? What god was present in the fray, when thou didst slay thy father, seizing him by the foot?"[1] In vii. 21, 7, mention is made of earlier gods: "Even the former gods admitted their powers to be inferior to thy divine prowess." And I apprehend that the two following verses, iv. 30, 3, 5, though otherwise rendered by Wilson (following Sâyaṇa), are to be understood of Indra fighting against the gods, and not with the gods, against the Asuras. 3. "Even all the gods assailed thee Indra, when thou didst prolong (?) day and night. 5. When thou didst fight alone against all the furious gods, thou didst slay the destructive." This interpretation is favoured by the tenor of verses 4, 6, 8–11 of the same hymn.[2] Earlier gods are also mentioned in x. 109, 4, though in conjunction with the seven rishis: "In regard to her the former gods said, the seven rishis who sat down to practise austerity," etc. An earlier age of the gods is mentioned in x. 72, 2, f.: "In the former age of the gods, the existent

[1] In explanation of this legend Sâyaṇa refers to the Taittiriya Sanhitâ, vi. 1, 3, 6. The following is the passage referred to, which I quote to show how little light it throws on the text of the R.V.:—*Yajno dakshiṇâm abhyadhâyat | tâm samabhavat | tad Indro 'châyat | so 'manyata "yo vâ ito janishyate sa idam bhavishyati" iti | tâm prâviṣat | tasyâ Indra evâjâyata | so 'manyata "yo vai mad ito 'paro janishyate sa idam bhavishyati" iti | tasyâ anumṛṣya yonim âchhinat | sâ sûtavaṣâ 'bhavat | tat sûtavaṣâyai janma | tâm haste nyaveshṭayata | tâm mṛgeshu nyadadhât | sâ kṛshṇavishâṇâ 'bhavat | "Indrasya yonir asi mâ mâ himsîr" iti* | "Yajna (sacrifice) desired Dakshiṇâ (largess). He consorted with her. Indra was apprehensive of this. He reflected: 'whoever is born of her will be this.' He entered into her. Indra himself was born of her. He reflected: 'whoever is born of her besides me will be this.' Having considered, he cut open her womb. She produced a cow." etc. No mention is made of his killing his father.

[2] I should observe that the Brâhmaṇas constantly speak of the gods and Asuras as being both the offspring of Prajâpati; as contending together (Ṣ. P. Br. v. 1, 1, 1; vi. 6, 2, 11; vi. 6, 3, 2); and even as being originally equal or alike (Sanskrit Texts, iv. 52). And to prove that even malignant spirits may be called "gods," Prof. Roth, *s.v. deva*, quotes from the Taitt. Sanh. iii. 5, 4, 1, a verse to the effect: "May Agni preserve me from the gods (*devâḥ*), destroyers of sacrificers, stealers of sacrifices, who inhabit the earth;" and a second text from the A.V. iii. 15, 5: "Agni, do thou through the oblation repel the gods who are destroyers of happiness" (? *sâtaghnaḥ*).

sprang from the non-existent. In the first age of the gods the existent sprang from the non-existent." See "Contribu-to a knowledge of the Vedic Theogony," etc., Journ. R.A.S., for 1864, p. 72; and compare Nirukta xii. 41,[1] where a former age or generation (?) of gods, *pûrvaṃ devayugam,* is referred to. I may add that A.V. vi. 64, 1, speaks of "former gods," and A.V. i. 30, 2, of some of the gods being fathers and some sons (*ye vo devâḥ pitaro ye cha putrâḥ.*) R.V. viii. 48, 13, speaks of Soma in concert with the Fathers, having "stretched out heaven and earth;" and x. 68, 11, of the Fathers having "adorned the sky with stars." But in these two passages the forefathers of the worshippers, supposed to have been raised to the rank of deities, may be meant. In R.V. x. 97, 1 (=Vâj. S. 12, 75; Nir. 9, 28; Ṣ. P. Br. 7, 2, 4, 26) mention is made of certain plants which were produced three ages (*triyugam*) before the gods.]

I have alluded above to the fact that Prof. Goldstücker does not always coincide with the interpretations proposed by Sâyaṇa. I will cite from his Dictionary a few further instances of this disagreement.

On the sense of "one who does not praise the deity with

[1] The verse which is illustrated in this passage occurs both in R.V. i. 164, 50, and in R.V. x. 90, 16, as well as Vâj. S. 31, 16. The concluding words are *yatra pûrve sâdhyâḥ santi devâḥ*, "where (in the sky) are the former Sâdhyas, gods." Yâska, as I mentioned above, tells us that the Nairuktas understood the Sâdhyas to be "the gods whose locality is the sky," *dyusthâno devagaṇaḥ*, whilst, according to a legend (*âkhyâna*), the term denoted a former age of the gods." Prof. Wilson translates the word Sâdhyâḥ by, "who are to be propitiated," a sense not assigned by Sâyaṇa, who proposes, first, that of *sâdhanâ yajnâdi-sâdhanavantaḥ karmadevâḥ*, "performers, performers of sacrifices, etc., work-gods." These words are rendered by Prof. Wilson in his note on i. 164, 50, "divinities presiding over or giving effect to religious acts." This does not, however, appear to be the real sense, as Mahîdhara on Vâj. S. 31, 17, tells us that "there are two kinds of gods, *karmadevâḥ*, "work-gods," and *âjânadevâḥ*, "gods by birth," the first being those who had attained to the condition of deities by their eminent works, and the second those who were produced at the beginning of the creation. The second class is superior to the first, and, according to the Brihadâraṇyaka, a hundred enjoyments of the latter (the work-gods), "are only equal to one single enjoyment of the former." See all this and more declared in the Bṛhadâraṇyaka Upanishad, pp. 817 ff. (p. 230 f. of translation), and Ṣatapatha Brâhmaṇa, p. 1087. The second sense proposed for *sâdhyâḥ* by Sâyaṇa on R.V. i. 164, 50, is that of the "deities presiding over metres," *chhando'bhimâninaḥ*, who, according to a Brâhmaṇa, by worshipping Agni were exalted to heaven, and became Âdityas and Angirases. Prof. Wilson remarks in his note: "It would seem that in Sâyaṇa's day the purport of the designation *Sâdhya* had become uncertain." Mahîdhara on Vâj. S. 31, 16, renders the term *virâḍ-upâdhi-sâdhakâḥ*, "producers of the condition of Virâj."

hymns," proposed for *amati*, he remarks (p. 343): "a doubtful meaning; it is proposed, besides the meaning 'poverty,' by Sâyaṇa on" (R.V. v. 36, 3).

On the word *amîvâ* he observes: "The same meaning (disease) applies satisfactorily to all other Vaidik passages where I have met with the word as a feminine; but Sâyaṇa has also the following interpretations, which seem artificial," etc.

On the alternative rendering of *amûra* by "combined with," etc., he remarks: "This meaning which is given by Sâyaṇa as an *optional one*, and the etymology on which it is founded by him, have little plausibility."

Under the word *ambi* he writes "(Ved.) water. Sâyaṇa holds that the word implies as well this meaning . . . as that of 'mother,' . . . so that it would express a double sense; but there seems to be no necessity to assign to it any other meaning than water."

Under *ayâ* he says: "Sâyaṇa here takes the instrum. *ayâ* as implying the *sense* of a genitive; . . . but it seems more probable that, as in other instances, some word, *e.g.* *âhutyâ*, etc., has to be supplied to it."

After giving under *ayâsya* the sense assigned by Sâyaṇa to that word, he observes, "but it seems that 'unable to be conquered,' might be more congenial with the context.

Under *araṇa* he remarks: "But Sâyaṇa has the improbable interpretation, 'unpleasant, painful;'" and again, "Sâyaṇa renders here *araṇa* in a very improbable manner, 'free from debt.'"

Under *aramati* he writes: "There seems no reason for adopting the other—rather artificial—meanings proposed by Sâyaṇa, and mentioned under ii. and iii."

Under *arari* iii. he says: "Both meanings appear to have been coined by Sâyaṇa for the sake of explaining the sense of *ararinda*."

If the principle that Sâyaṇa is open to free criticism of this description be admitted at all, the lengths to which dissent from his conclusions may be allowed to go must depend upon the discretion of the critic, and upon the philological principles which he adopts.

In rendering the particle *anâ*, "certainly," "indeed," Prof. Goldstücker *s.v.* departs from Sâyaṇa's explanation, at least in the only two places in which I have access to it, viz., R.V. iv. 30, 3, and viii. 47, 6, as on the former text he says it means *prâṇa-rûpeṇa balena*, "by strength in the shape of breath," and on the second that it signifies *prâṇa-yuktaḥ*, "possessed of breath." I am not aware how he renders it in x. 94, 3, 4.

Some apology is perhaps due to the Society for the long and minute examination into which I have entered of words and passages expounded by Yâska and Sâyaṇa. But it is evident that the only way in which a satisfactory estimate can be formed of the merits of any interpreter is by the presentation of such details. General assertions on such a subject, unless perceived to be founded on a sufficient induction of particulars carefully selected and thoroughly sifted, cannot be expected to command assent, especially if they run counter to opinions previously current.

It will be seen from the tenor of my observations that my object has not in general been to ascertain the true meaning of the words which I have discussed (though I have occasionally aimed at doing this), but to show either (1) that Yâska and Sâyaṇa are at variance with one another in regard to the sense of particular terms; or (2) that they have each given one or more alternative explanations of many words, and cannot therefore be supposed to have had in such cases any positive knowledge of the real signification; or (3), as regards Sâyaṇa, that he expounds numerous words differently in different places (without, as I presume, any justification of this variation in sense being in general discoverable in the context), and must, therefore, in some of those instances, at least, be held to have interpreted them wrongly.

From a consideration of these facts I am led to the conclusion that there is a large number of the most difficult words in the Rig-veda of the proper sense of which neither Yâska nor Sâyaṇa had any certain information, either from tradition or from etymology.[1]

[1] In regard to Indian tradition Prof. Benfey remarks as follows in note 160 to his translation of R.V. i. 51, 5, in his Orient und Occident: "If we compare

And this ignorance or uncertainty regarding the meaning of Vedic terms did not, as we have already seen, begin even with Yâska. It is clear from the preceding investigation that some important discrepancies in opinion prevailed among the older expositors, and the different schools of interpretation which flourished before his time. It has further been shewn that the Nighaṇṭus and the Nirukta are too limited in scope, as well, as in many instances, too general, or too uncertain, in their explanations, to serve as adequate helps for the elucidation of the hymns. The Nighaṇṭus, as we have found, do not expound nearly the whole of the obscure and obsolete words which they cite from the Veda, and the meanings which they do assign are often so vague as to leave us quite uncertain as to the specific signification of the terms. As we cannot tell for how long a period the hymns had ceased to be commonly understood, and particular words occurring in them had fallen into disuse before these vocabularies were compiled, it is possible that, in some cases, even the general meanings to which I have alluded may be incorrect, or, at least, may be different from those which the words had had in the earliest times. As regards the Nirukta, to say nothing of the fact formerly noticed, that it is but a very small portion of the hymns which it interprets at all, I think it is evident, from the instances I have given, that in the part which it does attempt to explain, the author depends very much upon etymological considerations for the senses he assigns; and this is made still more manifest by the fact of his frequently proposing two or more alternative or optional significations for the same word. Now it is possible that one or other of these explanations may be correct, or may be useful in suggesting the true sense; but the fact that Yâska offers us a choice of meanings seems to exclude the

the Indian interpretation, we recognize, as we have so often to do, how extremely little value we ought to attach to Indian explanations of words. On the other hand the correct explanation of things seems often to have been handed down, and such appears to be the case in the present instance."

On i. 61, 7, the same writer observes, note 614: "This is a strophe which is perhaps the best calculated to show how little use can be made of Indian tradition for the understanding of the Vedas, or rather how greatly it misunderstood them."

supposition that he had any certain knowledge, from tradition or otherwise, that any of them were entitled to the preference. No one, I presume, will imagine for a moment that the writers of the hymns had, as a general rule, more than one meaning in their minds.

As regards Sâyaṇa, it seems doubtful if he had any other authorities than those which he cites, such as the Brâhmaṇas (among which he mentions the Aitareya, Kaushîtakî, Taittirîya, Ṣatapatha, Ṣâtyâyana, Shaḍvinṣa, Tâṇḍya, and possibly others), the Âraṇyakas, the Nirukta, the Bṛhaddevatâ, etc. In his remarks on R.V. iv. 24, 9, he also refers to "ancient teachers acquainted with tradition" (*sampradâya-vidaḥ pûrvâ-châryyâḥ*), whose verses he quotes; and as we have seen above, he adduces in one place the name of Kapardin as authority for one of his interpretations. As he so frequently quotes the works in question to support his views, there is every reason to suppose that, in all important cases, he made it a practice to prove his point by reference to an older text, when ever he found one extant which could serve his purpose; and if so, we may generally infer that when he cites no such evidence, he had none to produce.[1]

The specimens which I have brought together of Sâyaṇa's defects and mistakes have been collected in the course of a few weeks from a very small portion of his voluminous work. It is therefore perfectly just to conclude that, if his whole commentary were carefully examined, it would be found to be pervaded throughout by faults of the same description. But although I have no doubt whatever that such is, in reality, the case, I will not be so unreasonable as to deduce from

[1] In as far as Sâyaṇa was in the habit of confining his view to the single text before him (which I admit was not always the case) the following curious passage (Nirukta pariṣishṭa 1, 12) which gives a just view of the principles of Vedic interpretation, might seem to have been written with a prophetic reference to his case, and conveys a lesson not altogether inapplicable even to Christian divines, who have been too much in the habit of expounding *their* sacred texts without reference to the connection. "This reflective deduction of the sense of the verses is effected by the help both of oral tradition and reasoning. The verses are not to be interpreted singly, but according to the context. For one who is not a rishi or a tapasvin has no intuitive insight into their meaning. . . . . . When the rishis were departing, men said to the gods, 'Who shall be our rishi?' The gods gave them this reasoning for a rishi," etc., etc.

these premises the sweeping conclusion which might be expressed in the words *ex uno disce omnia*, but will merely draw the more moderate and much fairer inference that there is no unusual or difficult word or obscure text in the hymns in regard to which the authority of the Indian Scholiast should be received as final, unless it be supported by probability, by the context, or by parallel passages. It follows, as a necessary corollary, that no translation of the Rig-veda which is based exclusively on Sâyaṇa's commentary can possibly be satisfactory.

It would, however, be preposterous to deny that there is a large proportion of his interpretations from which most material help can be derived; that his Commentary altogether has been of the utmost service in facilitating and accelerating the comprehension of the Veda; that it has made many things clear at once which it might otherwise have taken long and laborious investigation to discover: and that it ought to be constantly consulted before any interpretation based on etymology, on the context, or on comparison of parallel passages, is proposed. No reasonable man will deny this. It would be simply absurd to neglect any aid derivable from the productions of extant Indian scholarship.

After all, however, there is probably little information of value derived from Sâyaṇa which we might not, with our knowledge of modern Sanskrit, with the other remains of Indian authorship, and our various philological appliances, have sooner or later found out for ourselves. It is not easy to conceive that many important problems presented by Vedic antiquity could have long remained, or can now long remain, insoluble by the resources and processes of modern scholarship,—a scholarship which has already decyphered the cuneiform writings of Persia and the rock inscriptions of India, and discovered the languages which lay hid under those mysterious characters.

But whatever may be our obligations to Sâyaṇa or Yâska, there is no reason why we should stand still at the point to which they have conducted us, if we have the means of advancing further. If a pupil possesses advantages denied to former generations, it is surely unreasonable to charge him with presumption if he seeks to go beyond his master. It is no disparagement to Sâyaṇa, if those European scholars who have begun by taking him for their guide should be able gradually to improve upon his lessons, and should end by rejecting a good deal that they have learned from him, as erroneous. This is the natural course of science in general, and there is no reason why Vedic philology should be an exception.

There can, as it appears to me, be no doubt that the understanding of the Veda has been already materially promoted by the labours of Professor Roth and the other philologists who belong to the same school. That in some cases their proposed interpretations are erroneous, is, if true, no argument against the judicious application of the correct and scientific principles on which they profess to proceed. The new school has existed but for a very short time; the labourers connected with it are few; and it is not to be wondered at, if, in a novel and untrodden field, some mistakes should have been committed. The merits of a method are not to be estimated by the results which have attended the first essays of its advocates. These earliest attempts may have partially failed from want of skill or experience. Complete success can only be expected to follow the efforts of several generations of scholars. The interpretation of the Old Testament is a parallel case to that of the Vedic hymns. In how many passages of the Psalms and Prophetical Books does the sense still remain obscure and disputed, notwithstanding all that has been done for their elucidation by the critical acumen of Hebraists during several centuries!

All this is admitted by Prof. Roth, who, far from claiming infallibility for his opinions, thus expresses himself in the Preface to his Lexicon (vol i. p. vi.):—

"This part of our Dictionary, as it is the earliest, will also be the first to grow old, for the combined labour of many able scholars, whose attention is now directed to the Veda, will rapidly promote our understanding of it, and determine many things with greater truth and precision than was possible for us on our first attempt. Centuries have toiled at the lexicographical interpretation of Homer, and yet his vocabulary is not entirely explained, though, in point of language, Homer presents incomparably fewer difficulties than the Vedic hymns. How could people expect to transfuse, without delay, into other languages, these monuments of a remote antiquity which is preserved to us in writing nowhere else but here, just as if they were a piece of modern book-making?"

Prof. Roth has already given sufficient proof of his readiness to correct any interpretations which further research has led him to regard as erroneous. Compare the meanings assigned to *anṛtadeva* and *antideva* with the close of the article *deva*; *arâyî, âpântamanyu, krivi, nûnam, paritakmyâ*, as explained in his Lexicon, with the senses previously given to the same words in his Illustrations of the Nirukta, p. 62, p. 95, p. 96, p. 6, p. 151.

ON

THE RELATIONS OF THE PRIESTS

TO THE OTHER

CLASSES OF INDIAN SOCIETY

IN THE VEDIC AGE.[1]

By J. MUIR, Esq.

In a former paper on "Manu, the progenitor of the Aryan Indians," published in the Society's Journal,[2] I have attempted to shew that in general the authors of the hymns of the Rig-veda regarded the whole of the Aryan people, embracing not only the priests and the chiefs, but the middle classes also of the population, as descended from one common father, or ancestor, whom they designate by the name of Manu. This reference to a common progenitor excludes, of course, the supposition that the writers by whom it is made could have had any belief in the myth which became afterwards current among their countrymen, that their nation consisted of four castes, differing naturally in dignity, and separately created by Brahmâ.

That essay, however, leaves out of consideration any notices which the Rig-veda may contain regarding the different classes of which the society contemporary with its composition was made up. As this great collection of hymns embodies numerous references, both to the authors themselves and to the other agents in the celebration of divine worship, it may be expected to supply, incidentally or indirectly, at least, some

[1] This subject has been already treated in Professor Roth's book, Zur Litt. u. Geschichte des Weda; in his essay "Brahma und die Brahmanen," in the 1st vol. of the Journal of the Germ. Or. Society; in Dr. Haug's Tract on "the Origin of Brahmanism," and in the 1st vol. of my "Sanskrit Texts."

[2] Vol. xx. p. 406 ff.

information respecting the opinion which these ministers of religion entertained of themselves, and of the relation in which they stood to the other sections of the community. I shall now endeavour to shew how far this expectation is justified by an examination of the Rig-veda.

I have elsewhere[1] enquired into the views which the authors of the hymns appear to have held on the subject of their own authorship. The conclusion I arrived at was, that they did not in general look upon their compositions as divinely inspired, since they frequently speak of them as the productions of their own minds (*ibid.* pp. 128–140). But though this is most commonly the case (and especially, as we may conjecture, in regard to the older hymns), there is no doubt that they also attached a high value to these productions, which they describe as being acceptable to the gods (R.V. v. 45, 4; v. 85, 1; vii. 26, 1, 2; x. 23, 6; x. 54, 6; x. 105, 8), whose activity they stimulated (iii. 34, 1; vii. 19, 11), and whose blessing they drew down. In some of the hymns a supernatural character or insight is claimed for the Rishis (i. 179, 2; vii. 76, 4; iii. 53, 9; vii. 33, 11 ff.; vii. 87, 4; vii. 88, 3 ff.; x. 14, 15; x. 62, 4, 5), and a mysterious efficacy is ascribed to their compositions (Sanskrit Texts, vol. iii. pp. 173 f.) The Rishis called their hymns by various names, as *arka, uktha, ṛch, gir, dhî, nîtha, nivid, mantra, mati, sûkta, stoma, vâch, vachas*, etc. etc.; and they also frequently applied to them the appellation of *brahma*, as, for instance, in the whole, or most, of the following passages:—i. 31, 18; i. 37, 4; i. 61, 16; i. 62, 13; i. 80, 16; i. 117, 25; i. 152, 5, 7; i. 165, 14; ii. 18, 7; ii. 23, 1, 2; ii. 34, 6; ii. 39, 8; iii. 18, 3; iii. 29, 15; iii. 51, 6; iii. 53, 12; iv. 6, 11; iv. 16, 20, 21; iv. 22, 1; iv. 36, 7; v. 29, 15; v. 40, 6; v. 73, 10; v. 85, 1; vi. 17, 13; vi. 23, 1, 5; vi. 38, 3, 4; vi. 47, 14; vi. 50, 6; vi. 52, 2, 3; vi. 69, 4, 7; vi. 75, 19; vii. 22, 3, 9; vii. 28, 1, 2, 5; vii. 31, 11; vii. 33, 3, 4; vii. 35, 7, 14; vii. 37, 4; vii. 61, 2, 6; vii. 70, 6; vii. 72, 3, 4; vii. 83, 4; vii. 97, 3, 9; vii. 103, 8; viii. 4, 2; viii. 32, 27; viii. 51, 4; viii. 52, 2; viii. 55, 11; viii. 78, 3; viii. 87, 8; x. 13, 1; x. 54, 6;

[1] Sanskrit Texts, vol. iii. pp. 116—164.

x. 61, 1, 7; x. 80, 7; x. 89, 3; x. 114, 8. That in these passages *brahma* has generally the sense of hymn or prayer is clear from the context of some of them (as in i. 37, 4; viii. 32, 27, where *brahma* is joined with the verb *gâyata* "sing," and in vi. 69, 7, where the gods are supplicated to hear it), as well as from the fact that the poets are said (in i. 62, 13; v. 73, 10; vii. 22, 9; vii. 31, 11; x. 80, 7) to have fashioned or generated it, in the same way as they are said to have fashioned or generated hymns in other texts (as i. 109, 1; v. 2, 11; vii. 15, 4; viii. 77, 4; x. 23, 6; x. 39, 14), where the sense is indisputable; while in other places (iv. 16, 21; v: 29, 15; vi. 17, 13; vi. 50, 6; vii. 61, 6; x. 89, 3) new productions of the poets are spoken of under the appellation of *brahma*.

That *brahma* has the sense of hymn or prayer is also shown by the two following passages. In vii. 26, 1, it is said: "Soma not poured out does not exhilarate Indra; nor do libations without hymns (*abrahmâṇaḥ* = *stotra-hînâḥ*, Sâyaṇa). I generate for him a hymn (*uktha*) which he will love, so that like a man he may hear our new (production). 2. At each hymn (*uktha*) the soma exhilarates Indra, at each psalm (*nîtha*) the libations (exhilarate) Maghavat, when the worshippers united, with one effort invoke him for help, as sons do a father."[1] Again in x. 105, 8: "Drive away our calamities. With a hymn (*ṛchâ*) may we slay the men who are hymnless (*anṛchaḥ*). A sacrifice without prayer (*abrahmâ*) does not please thee well."

I have said that great virtue is occasionally attributed by the poets to their hymns and prayers; and this is true of those sacred texts when called by the name of *brahma*, as well as when they receive other appellations, such as *mantra*.

[1] It is clear from the context of this passage that *abrahmâṇaḥ* means "unattended by hymns," and not "without a priest." After saying that soma-libations without hymns are unacceptable to Indra, the poet does not add that he is himself a *priest*, or that he is attended by one, but that he generates a hymn; and the same sense is required by what follows in the second verse. Accordingly we find that Sâyaṇa explains *abrahmâṇaḥ* by *stotra-hînâḥ*, "destitute of hymns." The same sense is equally appropriate in the next passage cited, x. 105, 8. On iv. 16, 9, where *abrahmâ* is an epithet of *dasyu*, "demon," Sâyaṇa understands it to mean "without a priest," but it may mean equally well or better, "without devotion."

Thus it is said, iii. 53, 12, "This prayer (*brahma*) of Viṣvâmitra protects the tribe of Bharata;" v. 40, 6, "Atri with the fourth prayer (*brahmaṇâ*) discovered the sun concealed by unholy darkness;" vi. 75, 19, "Prayer (*brahma*) is my protecting armour;" vii. 33, 3, "Indra preserved Sudâs in the battle of the ten kings through your prayer, o Vasishṭhas." In ii. 23, 1, Brahmaṇaspati is said to be the "great king of prayers," and in v. 2 to be the "generator of prayers" (*janitâ brahmaṇâm*); whilst in x. 61, 7, prayer is declared to have been generated by the gods.

Brăhmăn in the masculine is no doubt derived from the same root as brăhmăn neuter, and though differing from it in accent as well as gender, must be presumed to be closely connected with it in signification, just as the English "prayer" in the sense of a petition would be with "prayer," a petitioner, if the word were used in the latter sense. As, then, *brăhmăn* neuter means a hymn or prayer, *brahman* in the masculine must naturally be taken to denote the person who composes or repeats a hymn or prayer. We do not, however, find that the composers of the hymns are in general designated by the word *brahman*, the name most commonly applied to them being *ṛshi*, though they are also called *vipra, vedhas, kavi*, etc. (see "Sanskrit Texts," vol. iii. pp. 116 ff.). There are, however, a few texts, such as i. 80, 1; i. 164, 35; ii. 12, 6; ii. 39, 1; v. 31, 4; v. 40, 8; ix. 113, 6, etc., in which the priest (*brahmâ*) may perhaps be understood as referred to in the capacity of author of the hymn he utters. So, too, in ii. 20, 4 and vi. 21, 8, a new composer (or, perhaps, merely a new reciter) of hymns is spoken of under the appellation of *nutânasya brahmaṇyataḥ*; in ii. 19, 8, the Gṛtsamadas are spoken of both as the fabricators of a new hymn (*manma navîyaḥ*) and as (*brahmaṇyantaḥ*) performing devotion; while in another place (x. 96, 5) Indra is said to have been lauded by former worshippers, *pûrvebhir yajvabhiḥ*, a term usually confined (as *brăhmăn* was frequently applied) in after times to the offerers of sacrifice. In three passages, vii. 28, 2; vii. 70, 5; and x. 89, 16, the *brahma* and *brahmâṇi* "prayer" and "prayers" of the *ṛshis* are spoken of; and in vii. 22, 9, *ṛshis* are said to have generated prayers (*brahmâṇi*). In i. 177, 5, we find *brahmâṇi kâroḥ*, "the prayers of the poet." The fact that in various hymns the authors speak of themselves as having received valuable gifts from the princes their patrons, and that they do not speak of any class of officiating priests as separate from themselves, would also seem to indicate an identity of the poet and priest at that early period. The term *brahman* must therefore, as we may conclude, have been originally applied (1) to the same persons who are spoken of elsewhere in the hymns as *ṛshi*, *kavi*, etc., and have denoted devout worshippers and contemplative sages who composed prayers and hymns which they themselves recited in praise of the gods. Afterwards, when the ceremonial gradually became more complicated, and a division of sacred functions took place, the word was more ordinarily employed (2) for a minister of public worship, and at length came to signify (3) one particular kind of priest with special duties. I subjoin a translation of the different passages in which the word occurs in the Rig-veda; and I have attempted to classify them according as it seems to bear, in each case, the first, second, or third of the senses just indicated. This, however, is not always an easy task, as in many of these texts there is nothing to fix the meaning of the term with precision, and one signification easily runs into another, as the same person may be at once the author and the reciter of the hymn.

I. Passages in which *brahman* may signify "contemplator, sage, or poet."

(In order to save the repetition of the word *brăhmăn* in parenthesis after *priest*, I have put the latter word in italics whenever it stands for *brahman*).

i. 80, 1.[1] "Thus in his exhilaration from soma juice the *priest* (*brahmâ*) has made (or uttered) a magnifying[2] (hymn)."

i. 164, 34. "I ask thee (what is) the remotest end of the

[1] I have to acknowledge my obligations to Professor Aufrecht for the assistance which he has freely rendered to me in the preparation of this paper, and especially in the translation of the more difficult texts which occur in the course of it.

[2] *Varddhanam* = *vṛddhi-karam stotram* (Sâyaṇa).

earth; I ask where is the central point of the world; I ask thee (what is) the seed of the vigorous horse; I ask (what is) the highest heaven[1] of speech. 35. This altar is the remotest end of the earth; this sacrifice is the central point of the world; this soma is the seed of the vigorous horse; this *priest* is the highest heaven of speech."[2]

ii. 12, 6. "He (Indra) who is the quickener of the sluggish, of the emaciated, of the suppliant *priest* who praises him," etc.

vi. 45, 7. "With hymns I call Indra, the *priest*,—the carrier of prayers (*brahma-vâhasam*),[3] the friend who is worthy of praise,—as men do a cow which is to be milked."

viii. 16, 7. "Indra is a *priest*, Indra is a rishi,[4] Indra is much and often invoked, great through his mighty powers."

x. 71, 11. (See the translation of the entire hymn below. The sense of *brahmâ* in v. 11 will depend on the meaning assigned to *jâta-vidyâ*).

x. 77, 1. (In this passage, the sense of which is not very clear, the word *priest* appears to be an epithet of the host of Maruts).

x. 85, 3. "A man thinks he has drunk soma when the plant (so called) has been crushed. But no one tastes of that which the *priests* know to be soma (the moon). 16. The *priests* rightly know, Sûryâ, that thou hast two wheels; but it is sages (*addhâtayaḥ*) alone who know the one wheel which is hidden. 34. The *priest* who knows Sûrya deserves the bride's garment."[5]

x. 107, 6. "They call him a rishi, him a *priest*, reverend, a chanter of Sâma verses (*sâma-gâm*), and reciter of *ukthas*,—he knows the three forms of the brilliant (Agni)—the man who first worshipped with a largess."

x. 117, 7. "A *priest*[6] who speaks is more acceptable than one who does not speak."

[1] Compare R.V. iii. 32, 10; x. 109, 4, below, and the words, "the highest heaven of invention."

[2] Compare R.V. x. 71 and x. 125.

[3] Compare *v.* 19 and stoma-vâhasaḥ, iv. 32, 12.

[4] Different deities are called *ṛshi*, *kavi*, etc., in the following texts: v. 29, 1; vi. 14, 2; viii. 6, 41; ix. 96, 18; ix. 107, 7; x. 27, 22; x. 112, 9.

[5] See Dr. Haug's Ait. Br., vol. i., Introduction, p. 20:

[6] The word here seems to indicate an order or profession, as the *silent* priest is still a priest.

(See Dr. Haug's remark on this verse, Ait. Br. Introd. p. 20; also the contexts of the two last passages in my article "Miscellaneous Hymns from the R. and A. Vedas," pp. 32 f.)

x. 125, 5. "I (says Vâch) make him whom I love formidable (*ugram*), him a *priest*, him a rishi, him a sage (*sumedhâm*)."

II. In the passages which follow the word *brahman* does not seem to signify so much a "sage or poet," as a "worshipper or priest."

i. 10, 1. "The singers (*gâyatriṇaḥ*) sing thee, the hymners (*arkiṇaḥ*) recite a hymn, the *priests* (*brahmâṇaḥ*), O Ṣatakratu, have raised thee up like a pole."

(Compare i. 5, 8; i. 7, 1; viii. 16, 9. See Dr. Haug's remark on this verse, Ait. Br. Introd. p. 20).

i. 33, 9. "Thou, Indra, with the believers, didst blow against the unbelievers, with the *priests* thou didst blow away the Dasyu."

i. 101, 5. "Indra, who is lord of all that moves and breathes, who first found the cows for the *priest*, who hurled down the Dasyu."

i. 108, 7. "When, o adorable Indra and Agni, ye are exhilarated in your own abode, or with a *priest* or prince (*brahmaṇi râjaṇi vâ*),[1] come thence, ye vigorous (deities), and then drink of the poured out soma."

i. 158, 6. "Dîrghatamas, son of Mamatâ, being decrepit in his tenth lustre, (though) a *priest*, becomes the charioteer of (or is borne upon) the waters which are hastening to their goal."

(Prof. Aufrecht understands this to mean that Dîrghatamas is verging towards his end, and thinks there is a play on the word "charioteer" as an employment not befitting a priest).

ii. 39, 1. "Ye (Aṣvins) are like two vultures on a tree; like two *priests* singing a hymn at a sacrifice."

[1] A distinction of orders or professions appears to be here recognized. In the following verse (v. 54, 7) a *rishi* and a prince are distinguished much in the same way as a *priest* and king are in i. 108, 7: "That man, whether rishi or prince, whom ye, O Maruts, support, is neither conquered nor killed, he neither decays nor is distressed, nor is injured; his riches do not decline, nor his support." Compare v. 14, where it is said, "Ye, O Maruts, give riches with desirable men, ye protect a rishi who is skilled in hymns (*sâma-vipra*); ye give a horse and food to Bharata, ye make a king prosperous." In iii. 43, 5, reference is found to Visvâmitra, or the author, being made by Indra both a prince and a rishi.

iv. 50, 7 ff. "That king overcomes all hostile powers in force and valour who maintains Bṛihaspati in abundance, who praises and magnifies him as (a deity) enjoying the first distinction. 8. He dwells prosperous in his own palace, to him the earth always yields her increase,[1] to him the people bow down of themselves,—that king in whose house a *priest* walks first[2] (*yasmin brahmâ râjani pûrva eti*). 9. Unrivalled, he conquers the riches both of his enemies and his kinsmen—the gods preserve the king who bestows wealth on the *priest* who asks his assistance."[3]

(The benefits resulting from the employment of a domestic priest (*purohita*) are also set forth in A.V. iii. 19, translated in my former article, "Miscellaneous Hymns from the R. and A. Vedas," in the volume of this Journal, p. 33).

iv. 58, 2. "Let us proclaim the name of butter (*ghṛta*), let us at this sacrifice hold it (in mind) with prostrations. May the *priest* (Agni ?) hear the praise which is chanted. The four-horned bright-coloured (god) has sent this forth."

v. 29, 3. "And, ye Maruts, *priests*, may Indra drink of this my soma which has been poured out," etc.

v. 31, 4. "The men[4] have fashioned a car for thy (Indra's) horse, and Tvashtṛ a gleaming thunderbolt, o god greatly-invoked. The *priests*, magnifying Indra, have strengthened him for the slaughter of Ahi."

v. 32, 12. "I hear of thee thus rightly prospering, and bestowing wealth on, the sages (*viprebhyaḥ*). What do the *priests*, thy friends, obtain who have reposed their wishes on thee, O Indra ?"

v. 40, 8. "Applying the stones (for pressing soma), performing worship, honouring the gods with praise and obeisance, the *priest* Atri placed the eye of the sun in the sky, and swept away the magical arts of Svarbhânu."

[1] Compare R.V. v. 37, 4 f.

[2] Compare viii. 69, 4; x. 39, 11; x. 107, 5; and the word *purohita*, used of a ministering priest as one *placed in front*. Prof. Aufrecht, however, would translate the last words, "under whose rule the *priest* receives the first or principal portion."

[3] See on this passage Roth's Art. on Brahma and the Brâhmans, *Journ. Germ. Or. Soc.*, i. 77 ff. See also Aitareya Brâhmaṇa, viii. 26.

[4] Ṛbhus ?

vii. 7, 5. "The chosen bearer (of oblations), Agni, the *priest*, having arrived, has sat down in a mortal's abode, the upholder."

vii. 33, 11. "And thou, o Vasishṭha, art a son of Mitra and Varuṇa (or a Maitravaruṇa-priest), born, o *priest*, from the soul of Urvaṣî. All the gods placed in the vessel thee, the drop which had fallen through divine contemplation."

vii. 42, 1. "The *priests*, the Angirases, have arrived," etc.

viii. 7, 20. "Where now, bountiful (Maruts), are ye exhilarated, with the sacrificial grass spread beneath you? What *priest* is serving you?"

viii. 17, 2 f. "Thy tawny steeds with flowing manes, yoked by prayer (*brahma-yujâ*),[1] bring thee hither, Indra; listen to our prayers. 3. We *priests*, offerers of soma, bringing oblations, continually invoke the drinker of soma."

viii. 31, 1. "That *priest* is beloved of Indra who worships, sacrifices, pours out libations, and cooks offerings."

viii. 32, 16. "There is not now any debt due by the active *priests* who pour out libations. Soma has not been drunk without an equivalent."

viii. 33, 10. "Look downward, not upward; keep thy feet close together; let them not see those parts which should be covered; thou, a *priest*, hast become a woman."

"viii. 45, 39. "I seize these thy tawny steeds, yoked by our hymn (*vacho-yujâ*) to a splendid chariot, since thou didst give (wealth) to the *priests*."

viii. 53, 7. "Where is that vigorous, youthful, large-necked, unconquered (Indra)? What *priest* serves him?"

viii. 66, 5. "Indra clove the Gandharva in the bottomless mists, for the prosperity of the *priests*."

viii. 81, 30. "Be not, o lord of riches (Indra), sluggish like a *priest*.[2] Be exhilarated by the libation mixed with milk."

viii. 85, 5. "When, Indra, thou seizest in thine arms the thunderbolt which brings down pride, in order to slay Ahi,

[1] Compare viii. 45, 39, below.

[2] Dr. Haug (Introd. to Ait. Br. p. 20) refers to Ait. Br. v. 34, as illustrating this reproach. See p. 376 of his translation. This verse clearly shows that the priests formed a professional body.

the (aerial) hills and the cows utter their voice, and the *priests* draw near to thee."

ix. 96, 6. "Soma, resounding, overflows the filter, he who is *priest* among the gods, leader among poets, rishi among the wise, buffalo among wild beasts, falcon among kites, an axe among the woods."

ix. 112, 1. "Various are the thoughts and endeavours of us different men. The carpenter seeks something broken, the doctor a patient, the *priest* some one to offer libations.[1]

ix. 113, 6. "O pure Soma, in the place where the priest, uttering a metrical hymn, is exalted at the soma sacrifice through (the sound of) the crushing-stone, producing pleasure with soma, o Indu (soma) flow for Indra."

x. 28, 11. (The word *brahmaṇaḥ* occurs in this verse, but the sense is not clear).

x. 71, 11. (See translation of this verse below, where the entire hymn is given).

x. 85, 29. "Put away that which requires expiation (?). Distribute money to the *priests*. 35. Behold the forms of Sûryâ. But the *priest* purifies them."

x. 141, 3. "With hymns we invoke to our aid king Soma, Agni, the Âdityas, Vishṇu, Sûrya, and Bṛhaspati, the *priest*.

III. In the following passages the word *brahman* appears to designate the special class of priest so called, in contradistinction to *hotri*, *udgâtri*, and *adhvaryu*.

ii. 1, 2 (=x. 91, 10). "Thine, Agni, is the office of *hotri*, thine the regulated office of *potri*, thine the office of *neshṭri*, though art the *agnidh* of the pious man, thine is the office of *praṣâstri*, thou actest as *adhvaryu*, thou art the *brahman*, and the lord of the house in our abode. 2. Thou, Agni, art Indra, the chief of the virtuous, thou art Vishṇu, the wide-stepping, the adorable, thou, o Brahmaṇaspati, art the *priest* (*brahmâ*), the possessor of wealth, thou, o sustainer, art associated with the ceremonial."

[1] This verse also distinctly proves that the priesthood already formed a profession. Verse 3 of the same hymn is as follows: "I am a poet, my father a physician, my mother a grinder of corn." Unfortunately there is nothing further said which could throw light on the relations in which the different professions and classes of society stood to each other.

iv. 9, 3. "He (Agni) is led round the house, a joyous *hotri* at the ceremonies, and sits a *potri*. 4. And Agni is a wife (*i.e.* a mistress of the house) at the sacrifice, and a master of the house in our abode, and he sits a *brăhmăn*."

x. 52, 2. "I have sat down an adorable *hotri*; all the gods, the Maruts, stimulate me. Day by day, ye Aṣvins, I have acted as your *adhvaryu;* the *brahman* is he who kindles the fire: this is your invocation."

I shall now bring forward the whole of the texts in which the word Brâhmăṇa, meaning a son, or descendant, of a *brăhmăn*, occurs in the Rig-veda.[1] They are the following:

i. 164, 45. "Speech consists of four defined grades. These are known by those Brâhmans who are wise. They do not reveal the three which are esoteric. Men speak the fourth grade of speech."

This text is quoted and commented upon in Nirukta xiii. 9.

vi. 75, 10. "May the Brâhman fathers, drinkers of soma, may the auspicious, the sinless, heaven and earth, may Pûshan preserve us," etc. etc.

vii. 103, 1 (= Nirukta 9, 6). "After lying quiet for a year, those rite-fulfilling Brâhmans[2] the frogs have (now) uttered their voice, which has been inspired by Parjanya...7. Like Brâhmans at the Atirâtra soma rite, like (those Brâhmans) speaking round about the full pond (or soma-bowl[3]),

[1] There are two more texts in which the word *brâhmana* is found, viz., i. 15, 5, and ii. 36, 5, on which see the following note. The word *brahmaputra*, son of a brahman, is found in ii. 43, 2: "Thou, O bird, singest a sâma verse like an *udgâtri*; thou singest praises like the son of a *brahman* at the libations."

[2] In the Nighantus, iii. 13, these words *brâhmaṇâ vrata-chârinaḥ* are referred to as conveying the sense of a simile, though they are unaccompanied by a particle of similitude. In his Illustrations of the Nirukta, p. 126, Roth thus remarks on this passage: "This is the only place in the first nine mandalas of the R.V. in which the word Brâhmaṇa is found with its later sense, whilst the tenth mandala offers a number of instances. This is one of the proofs that many of the hymns in this book were composed considerably later (than the rest of the R.V.). The word *brâhmana* has another signification in i. 15, 5; ii. 36, 5; and vi. 75, 10. (In the first of these texts, Roth assigns to the word the sense of the Brâhman's soma-vessel. See his Lexicon, *s.v.* It does not appear what meaning he would give to the word in vi. 75, 10. He has in this passage overlooked R.V. i. 164, 45, which, however, is duly adduced in his Lexicon). See Wilson's translation of the hymn; as also Müller's, in his Anc. Sansk. Lit. p. 494 f.

[3] *Saras.* See R.V. viii. 66, 4, quoted in Nirukta v. 11, where Yâska says, "The ritualists inform us that at the mid-day oblation there are thirty *uktha* platters destined for one deity, which are then drunk at one draught. These are here called *saras*." (Compare Roth's Illustrations on the passage.) See also R.V. vi. 17, 11, and viii. 7, 10, with Sâyana's explanations of all three passages).

you frogs surround (the pond) on this day of the year, which is that of the autumnal rains. 8. These soma-offering Brâhmans (the frogs) have uttered their voice, performing their annual devotion (*brahma*); these adhvaryu priests sweating with their boiled oblations (or in the hot season) come forth from their retreats like persons who have been concealed."

x. 16, 6. "Whatever part of thee any black bird, or ant, or serpent, or wild beast has mutilated, may Agni cure thee of all that, and Soma who has entered into the Brâhmans."[1]

x. 71, 1.[2] "When, o Bṛhaspati, men first sent forth the earliest utterance of speech, giving a name (to things), then all that was treasured within them, most excellent and pure, was disclosed through love.

2. = Nirukta iv. 10). "Wherever the wise,—as if cleansing meal with a sieve,—have uttered speech with intelligence, there friends recognize acts of friendliness; good fortune[3] dwells in their speech.[3]

3. "Through sacrifice they came upon the track of speech, and found her entered into the rishis. Taking, they divided her into many parts:[4] the seven poets celebrate her in concert."

4. (=Nir. i. 19.) "And one man, seeing, sees not speech, and another, hearing, hears her not;[5] while to a third she discloses her form, as a loving well-dressed wife does to her husband."

5. (=Nir. i. 20.) "They say that one man has a sure defence in (her[6]) friendship; he is not overcome even in the

[1] Compare A.V. vii. 115, 1 ff—xii. 5, 6.

[2] I cannot pretend that I am satisfied with the translation I have attempted of this very difficult hymn. Verses 4 and 5 are explained in Sâyaṇa's Introduction to the Ṛig-veda, pp. 30 f., of Müller's edition.

[3] I quote here as somewhat akin to this hymn another from the A.V. vi. 108, being a prayer for wisdom or intelligence. 1. "Come to us, wisdom, the first, with cows and horses; (come) thou with the rays of the sun; thou art to us an object of worship. 2. To (obtain) the succour of the gods, I invoke wisdom the first, full of prayer, inspired by prayer, praised by rishis, imbibed by Brahmachârins. 3. We introduce within me that wisdom which Ṛbhus know, that wisdom which divine beings (*asurâḥ*) know, that excellent wisdom which rishis know. 4. Make me, o Agni, wise to-day with that wisdom which the wise rishis—the makers of things existing—know. 5. We introduce wisdom in the evening, wisdom in the morning, wisdom at noon, wisdom with the rays of the sun, and with speech" (*vachasâ*).

[4] Compare x. 125, 3; i. 164, 45; (x. 90, 11); and A.V. xii. 1, 45.

[5] Compare Isaiah vi. 9, 10; and Matthew xiii. 14, 15.

[6] *Vâk-sakhye*, Yâska.

conflict (of discussion). But that person consorts with a vain delusion who has listened to speech without fruit or flower."

6. "He who abandons a friend who understands friendship, has no portion whatever in speech. All that he hears, he hears in vain, for he knows not the path of righteousness."

7. "Friends gifted both with eyes and ears have proved unequal in mental efforts. Some have been (as waters) reaching to the face or armpit, while others have been seen like ponds in which one might bathe."

8. (=Nir. xiii. 13.) "When Brâhmans who are friends strive (?) together in efforts of the mind produced by the heart,[1] they leave one man behind through their acquirements, whilst others walk about boasting to be priests." (This is the sense Prof. Aufrecht suggests for the word *ohabrăhmâṇaḥ*. Prof. Roth *s.v.* thinks it may mean "real *priests*." The author of Nirukta xiii. 13, explains it as meaning "reasoning *priests*," or "those of whom reasoning is the sacred science.")

9. "The men who range neither near nor far, who are neither (reflecting) Brâhmans nor yet pious worshippers at libations,—these, having acquired speech, weave their web imperfectly, (like) a female weaver,[2] being destitute of skill."

10. "All friends rejoice at the arrival of a renowned friend who rules the assembly; for such a one, repelling evil, and bestowing nourishment upon them, is thoroughly prepared for the conflict (of discussion)."

11. (Nir. i. 8.) "One man possesses a store of verses (*ṛchâm*); a second sings a hymn (*gâyatra*) during (the chanting of) the *ṣakvarîs*; one who is a *priest* (*brahman*) declares the science of being (*jâta-vidyâm*), whilst another prescribes the order of the ceremonial.[3]

R. V. x. 88, 19 (=Nir. vii. 31). "As long as the fair-

[1] Compare i. 171, 2; ii. 35, 2; vi. 16, 47.

[2] Such is the sense which Prof. Aufrecht thinks may, with probability, be assigned to *siris*, a word which occurs only here.

[3] According to Yâska (Nir. i. 8), these four persons are respectively the *hotri*, *udgâtri*, *brahman*, and *adhvaryu* priests. The brahman, he says, being possessed of all science, ought to know everything; and gives utterance to his knowledge as occasion arises for it (*jâte jâte*). See Dr. Haug's remarks on this verse. Ait. Br. Introd. p. 20.

winged Dawns do not array themselves in light, o Mâtarișvan, so long the Brâhman coming to the sacrifice, keeps (the fire), sitting below the hotri-priest."

(See Prof. Roth's translation of this verse in his Illustrations of the Nirukta, p. 113).

x. 90, 11 (= A.V. xix. 5, 6; Vâj. S. xxxi.). "When they divided Purusha, into how many parts did they distribute him? What was his mouth? what were his arms? what were called his thighs and feet? 12. The Brâhman was his mouth, the Râjanya was made his arms, that which was the Vaișya was his thighs, the Șûdra sprang from his feet."

(See the translation of this entire hymn in Sanskrit Texts, i. 6 ff.; and in my paper on "The Progress of the Vedic Religion," in Journal Roy. As. Soc. vol. i. new series, pp. 353 ff.).

x. 97, 22. "The plants converse with king Soma,[1] (and say), "for whomsoever a Brâhman acts (*kṛṇoti*, officiates), him, o king, we deliver."

x. 109, 1. "These (deities), the boundless, liquid Mâtarișvan (Air), the fiercely-flaming, ardently-burning, beneficent (Fire), and the divine primeval Waters, first exclaimed against the outrage on a *priest* (*brahma-kilbishe*). 2. King Soma,[2] unenvious, first gave back the priest's wife; Varuṇa and Mitra were the inviters; Agni, the invoker, brought her, taking her hand. 3. When restored, she had to be received back by the hand, and they then proclaimed aloud, 'This is the *priest's* wife;' she was not committed to a messenger to be sent:—in this way it is that the kingdom of a ruler (or Kshattriya) remains secured to him.[3] 4. Those ancient deities, the Rishis, who sat down to perform austerities, spoke thus of her, 'Terrible is the wife of the Brâhman; when approached, she plants confusion in the highest heaven.[4] 5. The Brahmachârin[5] (religious student) continues to perform observances.

[1] Compare *oshadhīḥ Soma-râjnīh*, "the plants whose king is Soma," in *vv.* 18 and 19 of this hymn.

[2] Compare R.V. x. 85, 8 f., 40 f.; and my contributions to Vedic Mythology, No. ii., p. 2 f.

[3] I am indebted to Prof. Aufrecht for this explanation of the verse.

[4] See R.V. i. 164, 34, 35, above.

[5] See my paper on the Progress of the Vedic religion, pp. 374 ff.

He becomes one member[1] of the gods. Through him Bṛhaspati obtained his wife, as the gods obtained the ladle which was brought by Soma. 6. The gods gave her back, and men gave her back; kings, performing righteousness, gave back the *priest's* wife. 7. Giving back the *priest's* wife, freeing themselves from sin against the gods, (these kings) enjoy the abundance of the earth, and possess a free range of movement."

This hymn is repeated in the Atharva-veda, with the addition of ten more verses, which I subjoin.

Atharva-veda, v. 17.

(*vv.* 1-3 = *vv.* 1-3 of R.V. x. 109).

4. "That calamity which falls upon the village, of which they say, 'this is a star with dishevelled hair,' is in truth the *priest's* wife, who ruins the kingdom which is visited by a hare attended with meteors."

(*vv.* 5-6 = *vv.* 5-4 of R.V. x. 109).

7. "Whenever any miscarriages take place, or any moving things are destroyed, whenever men slay each other, it is the *priest's* wife who kills them. 8. And when a woman has had ten former husbands not Brâhmans, if a *priest* (*brahmâ*) take her hand (*i.e.* marry her), it is he alone who is her husband. 9. It is a Brâhman only that is a husband, and not a Râjanya, or a Vaiṣya. That (truth) the Sun goes forward proclaiming to the five classes of men (*panchabhyo mânanebhyaḥ*."

(*vv.* 10-11 = *vv.* 6-7 of R.V. x. 109).

12. "His (the king's) wife does not repose opulent (*ṣatavâhî*) and handsome upon her bed, in that kingdom where a *priest's* wife is foolishly shut up. 13. A son with large ears (*vikarṇaḥ*) and broad head is not born in the house in that kingdom, etc. 14. A charioteer with golden neckchain does not march before the king's hosts (?)[2] in that kingdom, etc. 15. A white horse with black ears does not make a show, yoked to his (the king's) chariot in that kingdom, etc. 16. There is

[1] See A.V. x. 7, 1 ff., 9, 26.

[2] The word here in the original is *sûnânâm*, with which it is difficult to make any sense. Should we read *senânâm*?

no pond with blossoming lotuses in his (the king's) grounds in that kingdom where, etc. 17. His (the king's) brindled cow is not milked by his milkmen in that kingdom, etc. 18. His (the king's) milch cow does not thrive, nor does his ox endure the yoke, in that country where a Brâhman passes the night wretchedly without his wife."

I will now refer to a number of texts in which liberality to the authors of the hymns is mentioned with approbation.

Of these passages i. 125; i. 126; v. 27; v. 30, 12 ff.; v. 33, 8 ff.; v. 61, 10; vi. 27, 8; and vi. 47, 22 ff., may be consulted in Prof. Wilson's translation; and a version of R.V. x. 107 will be found in my article, "Miscellaneous Hymns from the Rig and Atharva Vedas," p. 32 f. The following are further instances:[1] —

vii. 18, 22 ff. "Earning two hundred cows and two cars with mares, the gift of Sudâs the grandson of Devavat and son of Pijavana, I walk about, as a priest does round a house, offering praises. 23. The four robust richly caparisoned brown[2] horses of Sudâs, the son of Pijavana, standing on the earth, carry me, son to son,[3] onward to renown in perpetuity." (See the translation of these verses in Roth's Litt. u. Geschichte des Weda, p. 100.) In i. 126, 3, and vi. 27, 8, also, the word *vadhûmantaḥ* is used as here, and is probably to be taken in the first of these passages of mares, and in the latter of cows, *vinṣatiṃ gâ vadhûmanto*, being "twenty bulls with their cows." The same sense of cows or mares is probably to be understood in viii. 19, 36. That the preced-

[1] The fourth volume of Professor Wilson's Rig-veda, edited by Mr. Cowell, having been published since this paper was written, the reader may compare his version of such of the following passages as are included in it with mine.

[2] The word here rendered is *smaddishṭayaḥ*. In his explanation of this passage Sâyaṇa considers it to mean *praṣastâtisarjanaṣraddhâdidânângayuktâḥ*, *i.e.* "possessing the approved constituents of a gift, viz., generosity, faith," etc. It occurs in three other texts, viz., in iii. 45, 5, as an epithet of Indra, where Sâyaṇa takes it to signify *bhadravâkya*, "speaking auspicious words;" in vi. 63, 9, where he takes it as = *praṣasta-darṣanân*, "of approved look;" and in x. 62, 9. Prof. Aufrecht considers the word to mean "strong," "robust," a sense which suits the context of iii. 45, 5 (where it cannot possibly bear the interpretation assigned by Sâyaṇa on vii. 18, 23), and apparently also that of x. 62, 9. From the etymology (apparently *smat* for *sumat*, "good" or "well," and *dishṭi*, "pleasure" or "good luck,") one would suppose it ought to mean "blessed" or "fortunate," a sense which might also suit the context of iii. 45, 5.

[3] *Tokaṃ tokâya.* The sense is obscure.

ing passages refer to the females of bulls or horses is made likely by comparing viii. 57, 17, which will be quoted below. In viii. 46, 37, however, reference is distinctly made to the gift of a woman (*yoshaṇâ*).

viii. 3, 21. "(The horse?) which Indra, the Maruts, and Pâkasthâman, the son of Kurayâṇa, gave to me, the most brilliant of all, like (the sun) careering in the sky. 22. Pâkasthâman gave me a tawny (horse) well broken in, and filling his traces, an indication of riches. 23. Like to which other ten swift steeds also bear the yoke, like those which carried the son of Tugra to his home. 24. Soul, food, body, raiment, the giver of vigour, and ornament—(all this Pâkasthâman is). I celebrate him as the fourth liberal bestower of a tawny horse."

viii. 4, 19. "We have celebrated among the Turvaṣus the profuse riches, consisting of hundreds of horses (bestowed) at the festivals of Kuranga, at the distributions made by this powerful and fortunate king. 20. After sixty thousand pure cows,[1] I, a rishi, have driven away herds of cattle obtained by the Priyamedhas with faces upturned to heaven, through the prayers of the sacrificing son of Kaṇva. 21. Even the trees[2] rejoiced at my arrival, (exclaiming), 'they have obtained cows in abundance, they have obtained horses in abundance.'"[3]

viii. 5, 37. "May ye, Asvins, take notice of my new gifts, how Kaṣu, of the race of Chedi, has bestowed on me a hundred camels and ten thousand kine. 38. The people are prostrate beneath the feet of the descendant of Chedi, and the men about him are but leather-workers (before him), who presented to me ten kings brilliant as gold. 39. Let no one try to walk in the path which these Chedis tread. No sage is regarded as a more bountiful man (than this prince." [4]

viii. 6, 46. "I have received a hundred from Tirindara, a

[1] Sâyaṇa explains *nirmajâm* as *niḥśesheṇa śuddhânam gavam*. Roth leaves the word unexplained; and Prof. Aufrecht suggests *nirṇijâm*, "garments," as perhaps the true reading.

[2] Compare Psalm xcvi. 12.

[3] This verse is translated in Benfey's Glossary in the Sâma-veda, *s.v. meha*.

[4] Or, "No one, (as) the sage expects, will (prove to be) a more munificent person."

thousand from Parṣu, the riches of the Yâdvas. 47. They gave three hundred horses, ten thousand cows, to Sâman the Pajra. 48. The exalted prince overpassed the sky, giving a yoke of four camels; he (overpassed) the Yâdva tribe by his renown."

viii. 19, 36. "Trasadasyu, son of Purukutsa, the bountiful lord, the patron of the virtuous, gave me fifty females (cows or mares).[1] 37. And while I was travelling . . . . at the ford of the Suvâstu, Ṣyâva, the wealthy lord of the Diyas (or of gifts) brought three seventies."

viii. 21, 17. "Was it Indra who gave to me, the worshipper, all this wealth? or was it the blessed Sarasvatî who gave this riches, or was it thou, Chitra? 18. King Chitra and other kings who (dwell) along the Sarasvatî, diffused himself (over us) like Parjanya, in a shower, bestowing a thousand and tens of thousands."

viii. 24, 29. "May the gift of Nârya reach the Vyaṣnas, offerers of Soma-libations, together with abundant wealth, in hundreds and thousands. 30. If any one, sacrificing, enquire of thee (o Ushas), wheresoever thou art engaged, where (he is), reply, 'This Vala dwells remote on the banks of the Gomatî.'"[2]

viii. 46, 21. "Let the ungodly man come forward[3] who has received as large a present as this which Vasa, the son of Aṣva, has received at the break of to-day's dawn from the Pṛthuṣravas, the son of Kanîta. 22. I have received the sixty thousand and ten thousand (appropriated to) the son of Aṣva, two thousand camels, ten hundreds of brown (mares), ten of (mares) with three ruddy spots, and ten thousand cows. 23, 24. Ten brown, impetuous, irresistible, swift, overbearing steeds of the bountiful Pṛthuṣravas, son of Kanîta, cause the circumference of the chariot wheel to whirl round. Bestowing a golden chariot, he has shewn himself a most bountiful sage, and acquired the most extended renown . . . . . . 30. As oxen approach the herd, so they

[1] See in note above the remarks on vii. 18, 22.
[2] Compare the similar expressions in R.V. v. 61, 19.
[3] This challenge seems to mean that no ungodly man had received such gifts.

draw near to me. 31. Then when he had called for a hundred camels from amongst the grazing herd, and two thousand among the white cattle, 32. I, the sage, received a hundred from the Dâsa[1] Balbûtha, the deliverer. These men of thine, O Vâyu, protected by Indra, rejoice; protected by the gods, they rejoice. 33. Then that large woman is led away, covered with jewels, towards Vaṣa, son of Aṣva."

viii. 54, 10. "May the opulent prince, who bestows on me speckled cows with golden housings, never perish, o gods. 12. Over and above the thousand speckled cows, I received a bright, large, broad, shining piece of gold. 13. Men have exalted to the gods the renown of the grandson of Durgaha,[2] who was bountiful to me in (bestowing) a thousand (cows)."

viii. 57, 14. "Near me stand six men in pairs, in the exhilaration of the Soma juice, bestowing delightful gifts. 15. Of Indrota I received two brown horses, from the son of Ṛksha two tawny, and from the son of Aṣvamedha two ruddy horses. 16. From the son of Atithigva (I received) horses with a beautiful car, from the son of Ṛksha horses with beautiful reins, and from the son of Aṣvamedha horses of beautiful form. 17. Along with Pûtakratu, I obtained six horses with mares[3] from Indrota, the son of Atithigva. 18. Among these brown horses was perceived a bay mare with a stallion, and with beautiful reins and a whip. 19. May no mortal, however desirous of reviling, fasten any fault upon you, o ye possessors of food."

x. 33, 4. "I, a rishi, have solicited king Kuruṣravaṇa, descendant of Trasadusyu, the most bountiful of sages. 5. Let me celebrate, at the (sacrifice), attended with a thousand gifts, (that prince) whose three tawny mares convey me excellently in a car. 6. Of which father of Upamaṣravas, the agreeable words were like a pleasant field to him who uttered them. 7. Attend, o Upamaṣravas, son (of Kuruṣravaṇa), and grandson of Mitrâtithi—I am the encomiast of thy father.

[1] Roth, *s.v. dâsa*, conjectures that instead of *dâse*, the proper reading is here *dâsân*, which would alter the sense to, "I received a hundred slaves from Balbûtha."

[2] Langlois *in loco* refers for illustration of this to R.V. iv. 42, 8.

[3] Sâyaṇa here understands *vadhûmataḥ*, of mares, *vaḍavâbhis tadvataḥ*.

8. If I had power over the immortals, or over mortals, my magnificent (patron) should still be alive. 9. The man even of a hundred years lives not beyond the period ordained by the gods;[1] so hath (everything) continually revolved."

x. 62, 6. "The Virûpas, who sprang from Agni, from the sky, Navagva, and Daṣagva, who perfectly possesses the character of an Angiras, is elevated to the gods. 7. The sages (princes) in concert with Indra lavished a herd of cows and of horses. Men have exalted to the gods[2] the renown of me, Ashṭakarṇî, who bestowed a thousand. 8. Let this man[3] now multiply; may he shoot up like a sprout, he who at once lavishes a thousand hundred horses for a gift. 9. No one equals him, as no one succeeds in grasping the summit of the sky.[4] The largesses of the son of Savarṇa have been diffused as widely as the sea. 10. Yadu and Turva gave two robust bondmen to serve (me) with abundance of kine. 11. Let not this man, the leader of the people, who lavishes thousands, suffer calamity. Let his largesses go on vying with the sun. May the gods prolong the life of the son of Savarṇa, from whom we, without fatiguing labour [or without cessation], have received food."

x. 93, 14. "I have spoken this (in praise) of Duhsîma, Pṛthavâna, Vena, and Râma,—a god among the magnificent,—who, having yoked five hundred (horses) for our benefit,—their (liberality) became renowned by (this) course. 15. Over and above this, Tânva straightway assigned, Pârthya straightway assigned, Mâyava straightway assigned (to us) here seventy-seven."

If we consider that the various texts which have just been quoted are the productions of the class whose pretensions they represent and whose dignity they exalt, and further, if we take into account the indications, supplied by various

[1] Compare R.V. viii. 28, 4: "As the gods desire so it comes to pass; no one—no mortal, however hostile—can hinder that (will) of theirs."

[2] Compare viii. 54, 12, above.

[3] In my article on "Manu, the progenitor of the Aryan Indians," Jour. R. A. S., xx. p. 416, note, I translated this word *manu* as a proper name, perhaps wrongly.

[4] Comp. Ṣ. P. Br. xiii. 5, 4, 14: "Neither former nor later men of the five races have reached this great work of Bharata (performed) to-day, as no mortal has reached the sky with his arms."

other passages which I shall cite below, of indifference to the gods and to their ministers manifested by the other sections of the community, we may think it necessary to make some deduction from the impression which we had at first received of the estimation in which the priestly order was held at the time when the hymns of the Rigveda were composed. But after every such allowance has been made, it will remain certain that the *brahman*, whether we look upon him as a sage and poet, or as an officiating priest, or in both capacities, was regarded with respect and reverence, and even that his presence was considered an important condition of the efficacy of the ceremonial. Thus, in i. 164, 35, the priest is described as "the highest heaven of speech;" in x. 107, 6, a liberal patron is called a rishi and a priest, as epithets expressive of the greatest eulogy; in x. 125, 5, the goddess Vâch is said to make the man who is the object of her special affection a priest and a rishi; in vi. 45, 7; vii. 7, 5; viii. 16, 7; and ix. 96, 6, the term "priest" is applied honorifically to the gods Indra, Agni, and Soma; in iv. 50, 8, 9, great prosperity is declared to attend the prince by whom a priest is employed, honoured, and succoured; and in iii. 53, 9, 12; v. 2, 6; vii. 33, 2, 3, 5; and vii. 83, 4, the highest efficacy is ascribed to the intervention and intercession of priests.

Again, although the commendations which are passed in the hymns on liberality to priests have been composed by interested parties, and though the value of the presents bestowed has no doubt been enormously exaggerated, there is no reason to doubt that the ministers of public worship, who possessed the gift of expression and of poetry, who were the depositaries of all sacred science, and who were regarded as the channels of access to the gods, would be largely rewarded and honoured.[1]

[1] It is to be observed that, in these eulogies of liberality, mention is nowhere made of Brâhmans as the recipients of the gifts. In two places, viii. 4, 20, and x. 33, 4, a rishi is mentioned as the receiver. In later works, such as the Ṣatapatha Brâhmaṇa, on the contrary, the presents are distinctly connected with Brâhmans. Thus it is said in that work, ii. 2, 2, 6: "Two kinds of gods are gods, viz., the gods (proper), whilst those Brâhmans who have the Vedic tradition, and are learned, are the human gods. The worship (*yajna*) of these is divided into two kinds. Oblations constitute the worship offered to the gods, and presents

It is further clear, from some of the texts quoted above (ii. 1, 2; iv. 9, 3; x. 52, 2), as well as i. 162, 5, and from the contents of hymns ii. 36; ii. 37; ii. 43; and x. 124, 1,[1] that in the later part of the Vedic era, to which these productions are probably to be assigned, the ceremonial of worship had become highly developed and complicated, and that different classes of priests were required for its proper celebration.[2] It is manifest that considerable skill must have been required for the due performance of these several functions; and as such skill could only be acquired by early instruction and by practice, there can be little doubt that the priesthood must at that period have become a regular profession.[3] The distinction of king or noble and priest appears to be recognized in i. 108, 7, as well as in iv. 50, 8, 9; whilst in v. 47, 7, 14, a similar distinction is made between king and rishi; and it is noticeable that the verse, in other respects nearly identical, with which the 36th and 37th hymns of the eighth mandala respectively conclude, ends in the one hymn with the words, "Thou alone, Indra, didst deliver Trasadasyu in the conflict of men, magnifying prayers" (*brahmâṇi vardhayan*); whilst in the other the last words are, "magnifying (royal) powers" (*kshattrâṇi vardhayan*), as if the former contained a reference to the functions of the priest, and the latter to those of the prince.

While, however, there thus appears to be every reason for supposing that towards the close of the Vedic period the priesthood had become a profession, the texts which have been quoted, with the exception of one (x. 90, 12) which will

(*dakshiṇâ*) that offered to the human gods, the Brâhmans, who possess the Vedic tradition, and are learned. It is with oblations that a man gratifies the gods, and with presents that he gratifies the human gods, the Brâhmans, who possess the Vedic tradition, and are learned. Both these two kinds of gods, when gratified, place him in a state of happiness" (*sudhâyâm*); (or "convey him to the heavenly world," as the expression is varied in the parallel passage of the same work, iv. 3, 4, 4)

[1] See also i. 94, 6, where it is said: "Thou (Agni) art an *adhvaryu*, and the earliest *hotri*, a *praśâstri*, a *potri*, and by nature a *purohita*. Knowing all the priestly functions (*ârtvijyâ*) wise, thou nourishest us," etc.

[2] See Prof. Müller's remarks on this subject, Anc. Sansk. Lit., pp. 485 ff.; and Dr. Haug's somewhat different view of the same matter in his Introd. to Ait. Br., pp. 11 ff.

[3] In regard to the great importance and influence of the priests, see Müller's Anc. Sansk. Lit., pp. 485 ff.

be further adverted to below, do not contain anything which necessarily implies that the priests formed an exclusive caste, or, at least, a caste separated from all other by insurmountable barriers, as in later times.[1] There is a wide difference between a profession, or even a hereditary order, and a caste in the fully developed Brahmanical sense. Even in countries where the dignity and exclusive prerogatives of the priesthood are most fully recognized (as in Roman Catholic Europe), the clergy form only a profession, and their ranks may be recruited from all sections of the community. So, too, is it in most countries, even with a hereditary nobility. Plebeians may be ennobled at the will of the sovereign. There is, therefore, no difficulty in supposing that in the Vedic era the Indian priesthood—even if we suppose its members to have been for the most part sprung from priestly families—may have often admitted aspirants to the sacerdotal character from other classes of their countrymen. Even the employment of the words *brâhmaṇa* and *râjanya* in the Rig-veda does not disprove this. The former word, derived from *brahman*, "priest," signifies, as already intimated, nothing further than the son or descendant of a priest (the word *brahmaputra*, "son of a priest," is, as we have seen, actually used in one text),—just as the latter (*râjanya*) means nothing more than the descendant of a king or chief (*râjan*).

The paucity of the texts (and those, too, probably of a date comparatively recent) in which the word *brâhmaṇa*

[1] Dr. Haug, in his tract on the "Origin of Brâhmanism," p. 5, thus states his views on this question: "It has been of late asserted that the original parts of the Vedas do not know the system of caste. But this conclusion was prematurely arrived at without sufficiently weighing the evidence. It is true the caste system is not to be found in such a developed state, the duties enjoined to the several castes are not so clearly defined as in the Law Books and Purâṇas. But nevertheless the system is already known in the earlier parts of the Vedas, or rather presupposed. The barriers only were not quite so insurmountable as in later times." This view he supports by a reference to the Zend Avesta, from which he deduces the conclusion that the people had been divided into three classes even before the separation of the Indian from the Iranian Aryans, and adds: "From all we know, the real origin of caste appears to go back to a time anterior to the composition of the Vedic hymns, though its development into a regular system with insurmountable barriers can be referred only to the latest period of the Vedic times." As thus stated, the difference between Dr. Haug and other European scholars is one of degree and age, not of principle, for none of them assert any distinction of race, or congenital difference, between the castes or classes.

occurs, when contrasted with the large number of those in which *brăhmăn* is found, seems to prove conclusively that the former word was but little used in the earlier part of the Vedic era, and only came into common use towards its close. In some of these passages (as in vii. 103, 1, 7, 8; x. 88, 19) the Brâhman is merely alluded to as a priest, and in vii. 103, the comparison of frogs to Brâhmans may seem even to imply a want of respect for the latter and their office.[1] In other places (i. 164, 45, and x. 71, 8, 9) a distinction appears to be drawn between intelligent and unintelligent Brâhmans, between such as were thoughtful and others who were mere mechanical instruments in carrying on the ceremonial of worship,[2] which, however, certainly points to the existence of a sacerdotal class. In another passage (x. 97, 22) the importance of a Brâhman to the proper performance of religious rites appears to be clearly expressed. In x. 109, where the words brăhmăn (*passim*) and brâhmaṇa (in *v.* 4) seem to be used interchangeably—the inviolability of Brâhmans' wives, the peril of interfering with them, and the blessing attendant on reparation for any outrage committed against them, are referred to in such a way as to shew at once the loftiness of the claims set up by the Brâhmans on their own behalf, and to prove that these pretensions were frequently disregarded by the nobles. In x. 16, 6, the Brâhmans are spoken of as inspired by Soma, and in vi. 75, 10, the manes of earlier Brâhmans are reckoned among those divine beings who have power to protect the suppliant. But in none of these texts is any reference made to the Brâhmans constituting an exclusive caste or race, descended from an ancestor distinct from those of the other classes of their countrymen. In fact, it is proved by one of the additions (cited above) which have been made in the Atharva-veda (v. 17, 8 f.) to one of the hymns just referred to (x. 10, 9), that, even at that later period when that addition was made, Brâhmans had but little regard to the purity of the sacerdotal blood, as they did not intermarry

[1] See Müller's remarks on this hymn in his Anc. Sansk. Lit., p. 494.

[2] In R.V. viii. 50, 9, it is said: "Whether an unwise or a wise man, O Indra, has offered to thee a hymn, he has gladdened (thee) through his devotion to thee."

with women of their own order only, or even with women who had previously lived single, but were in the habit of forming unions with the widows of Râjanyas or Vaiṣyas,[1] if they did not even take possession of the wives of such men while they were alive.[2] Even if we suppose these women to have belonged to priestly families, this would only show that it was no uncommon thing for females of that class to be married to Râjanyas or Vaiṣyas—a fact which would, of course, imply that the caste system was either quite unknown, or only beginning to be introduced among the Indians of the earlier Vedic age. That, agreeably to ancient tradition, Brâhmans intermarried with Râjanya women at the period in question, is also distinctly shewn by the story of the Rishi Chyavana and Sukanyâ, daughter of king Ṣaryâta, narrated in the Ṣatapatha Brâhmaṇa, and quoted in my former paper, "Contributions to a Knowledge of Vedic Mythology," No. ii., pp. 11 ff. See also the stories of the

[1] That the remarriage of women was customary among the Hindus of those days is also shewn by A.V., ix. 5, 27 f., quoted in my former paper on Yama, p. 299

[2] This latter supposition derives a certain support from the emphasis with which the two verses in question (A.V. v. 17, 8, 9) assert that the Brâhman was the only true husband. Whence, it may be asked, the necessity for this strong and repeated asseveration, if the Râjanya and Vaiṣya husbands were not still alive, and prepared to claim the restoration of their wives? The verses are, however, explicable without this supposition.

It is to be observed, however, that no mention is here made of Ṣûdras as a class with which Brâhmans intermarried. Ṣûdras were not Âryas, like the three upper classes. This distinction is not recognised in the following verse of the A.V. xix. 62, 1: Make me dear to gods, dear to princes, dear to every one who beholds me, both to Ṣûdra and to Ârya." (Unless we are to suppose that both here and in xix. 32, 8, *ărya* = a Vaiṣya, and not *ârya*, is the word.) In Ṣatapatha Brâhmaṇa, Kâṇva Ṣâkhâ (Adhvara Kâṇḍa, i. 6), the same thing is clearly stated in these words, for a copy of which I am indebted to Professor Müller:—*Tan na sarva eva prapadyeta na hi devâḥ sarveṇaiva sangachhante | ârya eva brâhmaṇo vâ kshattriyo vâ vaiṣyo vâ te hi yajniyâḥ | no eva sarveṇaiva samvadeta na hi devâḥ sarveṇaiva samvadante âryeṇaiva brâhmaṇena vâ kshattriyeṇa vâ vaiṣyena vâ te hi yajniyâḥ | yady enam ṣûdreṇa samvâdo vindet "ittham enam nichakshva" ity anyam brûyâd esha dîkshitasyopachâraḥ.* "Every one cannot obtain this (for the gods do not associate with every man), but only an Ârya, a Brâhman, or a Kshattriya, or a Vaiṣya, for these can sacrifice. Nor should one talk with every body (for the gods do not talk with every body), but only with an Ârya, a Brâhman, or a Kshattriya, or a Vaiṣya, for these can sacrifice. If any one have occasion to speak to a Ṣûdra, let him say to another person, 'Tell this man so and so.' This is the rule for an initiated man."

In the corresponding passage of the Mâdhyandina Ṣâkhâ (p. 224 of Weber's Edition) this passage is differently recorded.

From Manu (ix. 149–157; x. 7ff.) it is clear that Brâhmans intermarried with Ṣûdra women, though the offspring of these marriages were degraded.

Rishi Şyâvâşva, who married the daughter of king Rathaviti, as told by the commentator on Rig-veda, v. 61, and given in Prof. Wilson's translation, vol. iii. p. 344.

We have, however, still to consider the single text of the Rig-veda, x. 90, 11, 12, which seems at first sight to prove the existence of a belief in the separate creation of the four castes at the time when it was composed. A careful examination of the context in which these verses are found,[1] or even of the verses themselves, will, however, I think, lead to the conclusion that the representation is allegorical, and implies no opinion regarding the literal origination of the four classes. It is not even said that the Brâhman was produced from the mouth, the Râjanya from the arms, or the Vaişya from the thighs of Purusha; but that these classes formed respectively those members of his body. It is the Şûdra alone who is asserted to have sprung from the part of the body with which he is associated—the feet.

It is further to be noticed that as this hymn probably belongs to the close of the Vedic age, no conclusion can, on any interpretation of its meaning, be drawn from it in regard to the opinion regarding the different classes which prevailed in the earlier portion of that era. Dr. Haug, it is true, denies that the hymn is comparatively modern. He thinks that there is no sufficient evidence to prove this, but that, "on the contrary, reasons might be alleged to shew that it is even old." He is of opinion that the hymn had been used at human sacrifices, which he considers to have been customary in the earliest Vedic period, though they were afterwards abandoned as revolting to human feelings ("Origin of Brâhmanism," p. 5). Notwithstanding what is here urged by Dr. Haug, I cannot help agreeing with the opinion stated by other scholars, such as Colebrooke (Essays, i. 309, note; or p. 197 of Williams and Norgate's edition) and Max Müller (Ancient Sansk. Lit., p. 570 f.), that this hymn is of a later date than the great bulk of the collection in which it is found. As compared

[1] The entire hymn is translated in my paper on the Progress of the Vedic Religion, pp. 353 ff., and also in "Sanskrit Texts," vol. i. pp. 6 ff., where some remarks are made on it.

with by far the larger part of the hymns, it has every character of modernness both in its diction and ideas.

It is not denied that the hymns which we find in the Rig-veda collection are of very different periods. They themselves speak of newer and older hymns. So many as a thousand compositions of this sort could scarcely have been produced within a very short space of time, and there is no reason to imagine that the literary activity of the ancient Hindus was confined to the age immediately preceding the collection of the hymns. But if we are to recognize any difference of age, what hymns can we more reasonably suppose to be the oldest than those which are at once archaic in language and style, and naive and simple in the character of their conceptions; and on the other hand, what compositions can more properly be set down as the most recent than those which manifest an advance in speculative ideas, while their language approaches to the modern Sanskrit? These latter conditions seem to be fulfilled in the Purusha Sûkta, as well as in hymns x. 71; x. 72; x. 81; x. 82; x. 121; and x. 129. The pantheistic character of the opening parts of the Purusha Sûkta alone would suffice to demonstrate its comparatively recent date.

That even the legendary genealogies of the Purâṇas frequently assign to members of the four so-called castes a common origin, has been shown in my Sanskrit Texts, vol. i. chap. ii.; and for the evidence discoverable, both in the Rig-veda itself and in the epic poems and Purânas, that hymns were composed, and sacerdotal functions exercised, by persons who in later ages were called Râjanyas or Kshattriyas, as well as by Brâhmans, I may refer to the same volume, pp. 86–151 where the stories of Viçvâmitra and Devâpi are told.

In later times, when none but Brâhman priests were known, it seemed to be an unaccountable, and—as contradicting the exclusive sacerdotal pretensions of the Brâhmans—an inconvenient circumstance, that priestly functions should have been recorded as exercised by Râjanyas; and it therefore became necessary to explain away the historical facts, by inventing miraculous legends to make it appear that these men of the royal order had been in reality transformed into Brâhmans, as the reward of their superhuman merits and austerities (see Sanskrit Texts, vol. i., pp. 95 ff., 148 ff.). The very existence, however, of such a word as *râjarshi*, or "royal rishi," proves that Indian tradition recognized as rishis or authors of Vedic hymns persons who had belonged to Râjanya families. A number of such are named (though without the epithet of *râjarshi*) in the Anukramaṇikâ or index to the Rig-veda; but Sâyaṇa, who quotes that old document, gives them this title. Thus, in the introduction to hymn i. 100, he says: "Ṛjrâṣva and others, sons of Vṛshâgir, in all five râjarshis, saw this hymn in a bodily form (*sadehaṃ sûktaṃ dadṛṣuḥ*). Hence they are its rishis (or seers)." The 17th verse of this hymn is as follows: "This hymn the Vârshâgiras, Ṛjrâṣva, with his attendants Amvarîsha, Sahadeva, Bhayamâna, and Surâdhas, utter to thee, the vigorous, o Indra, as their homage;" on which Sâyaṇa repeats the remark that these persons were râjarshis. Ambarîsha is also said to be the rishi of ix. 98. Again, "Trasadasyu, son of Purukutsa, a Râjarshi," is said by Sâyaṇa on R.V. iv. 42, to be the rishi of that hymn. In the 9th verse Trasadasyu is thus mentioned: "Purukutsânî worshipped you, o Indra and Varuṇa, with salutations and obeisances; then ye gave her king Trasadasyu, a slayer of enemies, a demigod." Similarly Sâyaṇa says on v. 27: "Tryaruṇa son of Trivṛshṇa, Trasadasyu son of Purukutsa, and Aṣvamedha son of Bharata, these three kings conjoined, are the rishis of this hymn; or Atri is the rishi." As the hymn is spoken by a fourth person, in praise of the liberality of these kings, it is clear they cannot well be its authors. However, the Hindu tradition of their being so, is good proof that kings could, in conformity with ancient opinion, be rishis. Trasadasyu and Trayaruṇa are also mentioned as the rishis of ix. 110.[1] The rishis of iv. 43 and iv. 44 are declared by Sâyaṇa, and by the Anukramaṇikâ, to be Purumîlha, and Ajamîlha, sons or descendants of Suhotra. Though these persons

[1] In the Vishṇu Purâṇa, Trayyâruṇa, Pushkarin, and Kapi are said to have been sons of Urukshaya, and the last of them to have become a Brâhman. In the Matsya P., Trayyaruṇi, Pushkarâruṇi, and Kapi are said to have all become Brâhmans. (Wilson, V. P., p. 451, and note.)

are not said by either of these authorities to be kings, yet in the Vishṇu Purâṇa they are mentioned as being of royal race, and as grandsons of Suhotra, and according to the Bhâgavata P. a tribe of Brâhmans is said to have been descended from the son of Ajamîlha. In the sixth verse of iv. 44, the descendants of Ajamîlha are said to have come to the worship of the Aṣvins. The following hymns are said by tradition to have had the following kings for their rishis, viz.: x. 9, Sindhudwîpa, son of Ambarîsha (or Triṣiras, son of Tvashtṛ); x. 75, Sindhukshit, son of Priyamedha; x. 133, Sudâs, son of Pijavana; x. 134, Mândhâtṛ, son of Yuvanâṣva; x. 179, Sibi, son of Uṣînara, Pratardana, son of Divodâsa and king of Kâṣî, and Vasumanas, son of Rohidaṣva; and x. 148 is declared to have had Pṛthî Vainya as its rishi. In the fifth verse of that hymn it is said: "Hear, o heroic Indra, the invocation of Pṛthî; and thou art praised by the hymns of Venya." In viii. 9, 10, also, Pṛthî Vainya is mentioned among rishis: "Whatever invocation Kakshîvat has made to you, or the rishi Vyaṣva, or Dîrghatamas, or Pṛthî, son of Vena, in the places of sacrifice, take notice of that, o Aṣvins." Here Sâyaṇa refers to Pṛthî as the "royal rishi of that name."[1]

I have observed above that the contents of R.V. x. 109 not only display the high pretensions of the priestly order, but also indicate clearly that those pretensions were often disregarded by the ruling class. In fact, the hymns of the Rigveda contain numerous references to persons, apparently of different descriptions, who were either hostile or indifferent to the system of religious worship which the rishis professed and inculcated. We find there a long list of condemnatory epithets applied to these persons, such as *adeva*, *adevayu*, *anindra*, *abrahman*, *ayajyu*, *ayajvan*, *anyavrata*, *apavrata*, *avrata*, *devanid*, *brahmadvish*, etc., etc.; *i.e.*, "godless," "destitute of Indra," "without devotion," "unsacrificing," "following other rites," "averse to religious rites, or to law," "without rites, or lawless," "revilers of the gods," "haters of

[1] Even females are said to be authors of hymns or parts of hymns, as Romaṣâ, "daughter of Bṛhaspati, an utterer of hymns" (i. 126), Lopamudrâ (i. 179, 1), and Viṣvavârâ, of the family of Atri (v. 28).

devotion," etc. (i. 33, 3, 4; i. 51, 8, 9; i. 101, 2, 4; i. 121, 13; i. 131, 4; i. 132, 4; i. 147, 2; i. 150, 2; i. 174, 8; i. 175, 3; ii. 12, 10; ii. 23, 4, 8, 12; ii. 26, 1; iii. 30, 17; iii. 31, 9; iii. 34, 9; iv. 16, 9; v. 2, 9, 10; v, 20, 2; v. 42, 9, 10; vi. 14, 3; vi. 49, 15; vi. 52, 2, 3; vi. 61, 3; vi. 67, 9; vii. 6, 3; vii. 61, 4; vii. 83, 7; vii. 93, 5; viii. 31, 15 ff.; viii. 45, 23; viii. 51, 12; viii. 53, 1; viii. 59, 7, 10, 11; ix. 41, 2; ix. 63, 24; ix. 73, 5, 8; x. 22, 7 f.; x. 27, 1 ff.; x. 36, 9; x. 38, 3; x. 42, 4; x. 49, 1; x. 160, 4; x. 182, 3.) In most of these passages, no doubt, the epithets in question are connected with the words *Dâsa* or *Dasyu*, which—whether we understand them of barbarous aboriginal races, then partially occupying the Punjab, or of the evil spirits with which the darkness was peopled by the lively imagination of the early Indians—certainly did not ordinarily designate tribes of Aryan descent. But there are other texts containing denunciations of religious hostility or indifference, where no express reference is made to Dasyus, which may with more or less probability be understood of members of the Aryan community. Such are the following:—

i. 84, 7. "Indra, who alone distributes riches to the sacrificing mortal, is lord and irresistible. 7. When will Indra crush the illiberal (*arâdhasam*) man like a bush with his foot? when will he hear our hymns?"

i. 101, 4. "Indra, who is the slayer of him, however strong, who offers no libations."

i. 122, 9. "The hostile man, the malicious enemy, who pours out no libations to you, o Mitra and Varuṇa, plants fever in his own heart, when the pious man has by his offerings obtained (your blessing)."

i. 124, 10. "Wake, o magnificent Dawn (Ushas), the men who present offerings; let the thoughtless niggards (*paṇayaḥ*)[1] sleep." (Comp. iv. 51, 3.)

1. 125, 7. "Let not the liberal suffer evil or calamity; let not devout sages decay; let them have some further term; let griefs befall the illiberal (*apṛṇantam*)."

[1] This sense of the word is confirmed by i. 33, 3, where the rishi says to Indra, "*mâ paṇir bhûr asmad adhi*," "Be not niggardly towards us."

i. 147, 2. "One man contemns (*pîyati*), whilst another praises, thee. Reverent, I adore thy manifestation, o Agni."

i. 176, 4. "Slay every one who offers no oblations—though difficult to destroy[1]—who is displeasing to thee. Give us his wealth; the sage expects it."

i. 182, 3. "What do ye here, o powerful (Aṣvins)? Why do ye sit in the house of any man who offers no sacrifice, and yet is honoured? Assail, wear away the breath of the niggard (*paṇer asum*), and create light for the sage who desires to praise you."

i. 190, 5. "Those persons who, flourishing, but wicked, regarding thee, o god, as a feeble being, depend upon thee who art gracious—thou bestowest nothing desirable upon the malignant, thou, o Bṛhaspati, avengest thyself on the scorner (*piyârum*)."

ii. 23, 4. "By thy wise leadings thou guidest and protectest the man who worships thee: no calamity can assail him who hates devotion (*brahma-dvishaḥ*), and the queller of his wrath: this, o Bṛhaspati, is thy great glory."

ii. 26, 1. "The upright worshipper shall slay those who seek to slay (him); the godly shall overcome the ungodly; the religious shall slay in battle even him who is hard to conquer; the sacrificer shall divide the spoils of the unsacrificing."

iv. 24, 2. "In battle Indra bestows riches upon the man who offers prayers (*brahmaṇyate*) and libations. . . . . . . 5. Then some men worship the mighty (Indra); then the cooker of oblations will present his offering of meal; then Soma will abandon those who offer no libations; then (the impious) will be fain to worship the vigorous (god)."

iv. 25, 5. "Dear is the righteous man, dear to Indra is the man who reveres him, dear is the worshipper, dear to him is the offer of soma. 6. This impetuous and heroic Indra regards as peculiarly his own the cooked oblation of the devout soma-offerer; he is not the relation, or friend, or kinsman, of the man who offers no libations; he destroys the prostrate irreligious man. 7. Indra, the soma-drinker, approves not

[1] Roth, *s.v.* understands *dûṇâṣam* to mean "continually."

friendship with the wealthy niggard (*revatâ paṇinâ*) who offers no libations. He deprives him of his riches, and destroys him when stripped bare, whilst he is the exclusive favourer of the man who offers libations and cooks offerings."

iv. 51, 3. "The magnificent dawns, appearing, have to-day aroused the liberal to the bestowal of wealth. Let the niggards (*paṇayaḥ*) sleep in gloom, and the regardless in the midst of darkness." (Compare i. 124, 10.)

v. 34, 3 (= Nirukta vi. 19). "Whoever offers soma-libations to Indra, either in sunshine or darkness, becomes glorious. The mighty god drives away the ostentatious; the opulent god (drives away) the man who decks out his person, and is the friend of the degraded. (Yâska adds to these epithets of the objects of Indra's enmity that of *ayajvânam*, 'one who does not worship.') 5. Indra desires no support from five or from ten (allies); he consorts not with the man who offers no libation, however flourishing; but overwhelms, and at once destroys such a person, whilst he gives the godly man a herd of kine as his portion. 6. . . . . The enemy of him who makes no libations, the promoter of him who offers libations, Indra, the terrible subduer of all, the lord, brings the Dâsa into subjection. 7. He gathers together the goods of the niggard (*paṇeḥ*) to be spoiled; he allots to the sacrificer wealth beneficial for men. Every one who provokes his fury is deeply involved in difficulty."

v. 42, 7. "Praise the first depositary of gems, Brihaspati, the bestower of riches, who is most propitious to the man that hymns and lauds him, who comes with abundant wealth to the man that invokes him. 8. Those who are attended by thy succours, Brihaspati, are unharmed, affluent, rich in men. The possessions of those who bestow horses, cows, and raiment, are blest. 9. Make unblest the wealth of those who enjoy themselves while they do not gratify (thee) with our hymns.[1] Drive away from the sunlight those haters of devotion (*brahma-dvishaḥ*) who are averse to religious rites, while they increase in progeny. 10. Hasten, o Maruts, with-

[1] Or, according to Sâyaṇa, "who do not satisfy us who are possessed of laudatory hymns."

out wheels[1] against the man who attends at the sacrifice of a Rakshas (or sinner).[2] He who reviles the man who celebrates your service secures but contemptible pleasures, however much he may sweat."

vi. 13, 3. "That lord of the virtuous by his power destroys Vrittra (or the enemy); o wise Agni, offspring of the ceremonial, that sage whom thou in concert with the son of the waters prosperest with wealth, divides the spoil of the niggard (*paṇeḥ*)."

vi. 44, 11. "Abandon us not, o vigorous god, to the destroyer; let us not suffer injury whilst we live in the friendship of thee who art opulent. Thy former bounties to men (are known); slay those who offer no libations; root out the illiberal (*apṛṇataḥ*)."

vi. 52, 1. "By heaven or by earth I approve not that, nor by (this) sacrifice, nor by these rites.[3] Let the strong mountains crush him; let the priest (*yashṭâ*) of Atiyâja fall. 2. Whoever, o Maruts, regards himself as superior to us, or reviles our worship when performed, may scorching calamities light upon him; may the sky consume that hater of devotion (*brahma-dvisham*).[4] 3. Why, o Soma, do they call thee the protector of devotion, or our preserver from imprecations? Why doest thou see us reviled? Hurl thy burning bolt against the hater of devotion (*brahma-dvishe*)." (These verses perhaps refer to the struggles of rival priests. Professor Aufrecht renders the words *atiyâjasya yashṭâ*, by "he who tries to outdo us in sacrifices." Sâyaṇa, who is followed by Professor Goldstücker, makes *atiyâja* the name of a rishi. Professor Roth takes it to mean "very pious.")

vi. 53, 3. "Impel to liberality, o burning Pûshan, even

[1] *Achakrebhiḥ*, easily, swiftly, noiselessly, suddenly. Compare the phrase *achakrayâ svadhayâ vartamânam* in x. 27, 19, and *nichakrayâ*, viii. 7, 29.

[2] This latter rendering of the words *ya ohate rakshaso devavitau*, is suggested by Professor Aufrecht. Compare the words *mâ no martâya ripave rakshasvine*, etc., viii. 49, 8, and *yo naḥ kaşchid ririkshati rakshastvena martyaḥ*, etc., viii. 18, 13. Sâyaṇa renders the words under consideration by "who brings Rakshases to to the sacrifice,—by irregular observances, etc., makes it demoniacal (*âsura*)."

[3] The sense of this is not very clear, unless, as Professor Aufrecht proposes, we understand the words as an oath.

[4] This verse occurs in a modified form in the A.V. ii. 12, 6, but without any perceptible difference of sense.

the man who wishes to give nothing. Soften[1] the soul even of the niggard (*paṇeḥ*). 4. Open up paths by which we may obtain food; slay our enemies; let our ceremonies be successful, o terrible god. 5. O wise deity, pierce the hearts of the niggards (*paṇînâm*) with a probe; and then subject them to us. 6. Pierce them with a goad, o Pûshan; seek (for us) that which is dear to the heart of the niggard (*paṇeḥ*); and then subject them to us. 7. Penetrate and tear the hearts of the niggards (*paṇînâm*), o wise deity, and then subject them to us. 8. With that prayer-promoting probe (*brahmachodinîm ârâm*) which thou holdest, o burning Pûshan, penetrate and tear the heart of every (such man)."

vii. 83, 4. "O Indra and Varuṇa, unrivalled with your weapons, slaying Bheda, ye preserved Sudâs; ye listened to the prayers of these men in the battle; the priestly office of the Tritsus proved efficacious. . . . . 6. Both invoke you, Indra and Varuṇa, for the acquisition of spoil (as) in the conflicts where ye protected Sudâs with the Tritsus, when he was assailed by the ten kings. 7. Ten unsacrificing (*ayajyavaḥ*) kings did not, o Indra and Varuṇa, vanquish Sudâs. The praises of the men who partake in the sacrificial feast were effectual; the gods were present at their invocations. 8. O Indra and Varuṇa, ye gave succour to Sudâs when surrounded in the battle of the ten kings, where the devout white-robed Tritsus, with knotted hair, worshipped you with reverence and prayer."

[In the first verse of this hymn Indra and Varuṇa are said to have slain both the Dâsa and Ârya enemies of Sudâs. His enemies were therefore in part Âryas, and the ten kings alluded to in the verses I have quoted were no doubt of this race. And yet it is to be observed that in *v.* 7 they are described as *ayajyavaḥ*, "unsacrificing." If, therefore, this expression is to be taken literally, it would follow that these Aryan kings were not worshippers of Indra and Varuṇa. Perhaps, however, the epithet is only to be understood in a general way, as meaning "ungodly." If we are to take the indefinite word "both" (*ubhayâsah*) in verse 6, as meaning

[1] Or, "crush" (*vi mrada*).

"both the contending hosts," it would, indeed, result that not only Sudâs but also the ten kings who were fighting against him offered supplications to the same gods; but this would seem to be in contradiction to the literal sense of the word "unsacrificing" in the following verse; and Sâyaṇa understands "both" to refer to Sudâs and the Tritsus who were his helpers].

vii. 19, 1. "Who (Indra) bestows on the man who offers many libations the wealth of the family which does not worship (him)."

viii. 2, 18. The gods love a man who offers oblations; they do not approve sleep. The active obtain delight." (Compare viii. 86, 3).

viii. 14, 15. "Thou, o Indra, a drinker of soma, who art supreme, hast scattered and destroyed the hostile assembly which offers no oblations."

viii. 31, 15. "Impetuous is the chariot of the godly man, and he is a hero in every battle. The sacrificer who seeks to please the gods overcomes the man who does not sacrifice. 16. Thou dost not perish, o sacrificer, nor thou, o offerer of libations, nor thou, o godly man."

viii. 45, 15. "Bring to us the wealth of the man who, being rich, but no sacrificer, refuses to present offerings. . . . 23. Let not violent fools, let not deriders insult thee. Love not the haters of devotion (*brahmadvishaḥ*)."

viii. 51, 12. "Let us praise Indra truly, not falsely. Great destruction overtakes the man who offers no libations, whilst he who offers them has many lights."

viii. 53, 1. "Let our hymns exhilarate thee; give us wealth, o Thunderer. Slay the haters of devotion (*brahmadvishaḥ*). 2. Crush with thy foot the niggards (*paṇīn*), who bestow nothing;[1] thou art great; no one equals thee."

viii. 59, 7. "O long-lived god, the ungodly man shall not obtain food. . . . . 10. Thou, Indra, lovest our rites; thou satiatest (? ironically) those who revile thee. . . . ." Perhaps these expressions may refer to the Dâsas and Dasyu, who are mentioned in the context.

[1] In ix. 101, 13, we find *śvânam arâdhasam*, "the dog who bestows nothing."

viii. 86, 2. "Bestow, o Indra, upon the worshipper who offers libations and gives presents, and not upon the niggard (*paṇau*), the horse and cow which thou possessest, as an undecaying portion. 3. Let the godless man who performs no rites, and sleeps an incessant sleep, destroy by his own acts[1] the wealth which sustains him; sever him from it."

x. 27, 1. "The impulse comes upon me (says Indra) to bestow (blessings) on the sacrificer who offers libations. I slay the man who utters no praises, who is an enemy of truth, a sinner, and empty."[2]

x. 32. "May the (worshippers) who constantly bring thee to the sacrifices slay the boasters (or talkers) who give no presents" (*vagvanân arâdhasaḥ*).

x. 38, 3. "Whatever godless man (*adevaḥ*), whether Dâsa or Ârya, o much-lauded Indra, seeks after us to vanquish us, let these enemies be easy for us to overcome; through thee may we slay them in the conflict."

[This passage shows that Âryas as well as Dâsas were charged with being deniers of the Aryan gods (compare vii. 83, 7); unless we are to consider the term "godless" as employed, as in modern times,[3] to describe persons who were practically, though not theoretically, unbelievers. This latter view is confirmed by A.V. v. 8, 3, where an enemy plotting against the worshipper, and employing a *priest* (*v.* 5), is yet described as "godless."]

x. 42, 4. . . "Here the hero (Indra) takes for a friend the man who brings offerings; he desires no friendship with the man who pours out no libations."

x. 49, 1. . . "I (says Indra) bestow the earliest riches on the man who praises me: I have made for myself a hymn which magnifies me. I am the encourager of the man who sacrifices. I overwhelm in every conflict those who do not sacrifice."

x. 160, 4. "Whoever, loving the gods, offers libations of soma to Indra with an ardent soul, with his whole heart,—Indra does not give up his kine (to spoliation), but makes for

[1] Compare viii. 18, 13.

[2] "Empty-handed," *ábhum*, as explained by Böhtlingk and Roth *s.v.*

[3] *e.g.* in the case of the Government Colleges in Ireland.

him (the soma-libation) approved and pleasing.[1] 4. That man is observed by Indra who, though rich, offers to him no libations of soma. Maghavat grasps him in his fist,[2] and slays the haters of devotion (*brahmadvishaḥ*) though unsolicited."

That the wealthy man here referred to is an Âryan is rendered probable by the tenor of the following text, where the rich man there alluded to, after contemning Indra during a period of security, concludes by invoking the god when he has been terrified into devotion by the manifestations of his power and anger:

viii. 21, 14. "Thou takest not a rich man for thy friend. Drunkards contemn thee. When thou utterest a sound, and musterest (thy hosts), then thou art invoked as a father."[3]

[1] Prof. Aufrecht suggested that the words "the soma libation," should be understood in this verse, and compares vii. 84, 3, and x. 39, 2. The blessings which attend a devout worshipper of Indra are also described in vi. 28, 2 ff.

[2] See Prof. Goldstücker's Sanskrit Lexicon *s.v. aratni*. Sâyaṇa's interpretation of this verse, as there quoted and translated by Prof. G., is as follows: "Indra manifests himself (to the pious); (the sacrificer), who, though not wealthy, offers him the soma libation,—him, Indra, the wealthy, holds in his hand (lit. *fist*, *i.e.* he protects him), after having defeated (*niḥ* scil. *kṛshya*) his enemies; even unsolicited he slays the foes of the Brâhmans." I am, I confess, bold enough to consider the rendering I have given in the text as preferable to Sâyaṇa's in the parts where mine differs from his. His connection of the negative particle *na* which follows *revân* with that word (so as to make it = *arevân*), instead of with the verb *sunoti*, seems forced and unnatural, especially as rich men are often censured as non-sacrificers (as in iv. 25, 7; v. 34, 5, v. 42, 9; viii. 45, 15). Prof. Roth conjecturally interprets *aratnau nirdadhâti* as meaning "he finds him out in a corner." Prof. Aufrecht would render, "holds him at arm's length, despises him."

[3] Compare the following additional passages:—i. 110, 7; i. 113, 18; i. 121, 13; i. 131, 4; i. 132, 4; i. 133, 7; i. 151, 7; i. 152, 2; i. 174, 6; vi. 22, 8; vi. 23, 2, 3, 9. We read in i. 51, 8: "Distinguish between the Âryas and those who are Dasyus; chastising the men who are destitute of rites (or lawless), subject them to the sacrificer. Be a strong supporter of thy worshipper," etc.; and in i. 130, 8: "Indra preserved the sacrificing Ârya in battle." But it does not follow from such texts that the Âryas are always identifiable with the worshippers of the gods, though the two classes would generally include the same persons.

As the people named in the following verse (iii. 53, 14), the Kîkaṭas, seem to have lived on the outskirts of Âryan civilization, no conclusion can be drawn from it in reference to the point before us. "What are thy cows, (o Indra) doing among the Kîkaṭas? (These people) neither draw (from these cows) milk to mix with the soma, nor do they heat the sacrificial kettle. Bring to us the wealth of Pramaganda (or the usurer); subject to us the degraded people." The Kîkaṭas, according to Yâska (Nir. vi. 32), are a non-Âryan race; though he and Sâyaṇa give *nâstikas* or atheists as an alternative sense. Prof. Weber (Indische Studien, i. 186) thinks that as Kîkaṭa is an old name for Magadha or Behar, we may understand the word *anâryya* used by Yâska as meaning an Âryan tribe which

(See "Contributions to Vedic Theogony," etc., p. 101, note 1.) In vi. 47, 16, Indra is said to be the enemy of the prosperous man (*edhamânadviṭ*), probably an Ârya who rendered him no service.[1]

In two other passages we are even told that doubts were entertained by some in regard to Indra's existence; ii. 12, 5: "Have faith in that terrible being of whom men ask 'where is he?' and declare that he is not. He destroys the possessions of the foe, etc. . . . . 15. Thou art true, who being irresistible, continually providest food for him who pours out libations and cooks oblations."

viii. 89, 3. "Seeking food, present a hymn to Indra, a true hymn, if he truly exists. 'Indra does not exist,' says some one; 'who has seen him? whom shall we praise?' 'This is I, o worshipper (exclaims Indra), behold me here, I surpass all beings in greatness.'"

It seems evident from the preceding texts that the *parcus deorum cultor et infrequens* was by no means a rare character among the Âryas of the Vedic age, and that the priests found no little difficulty in drawing forth the liberality of their lay contemporaries towards themselves, and in enforcing a due regard to the ceremonials of devotion. It would even appear that the ministers of religion had to encounter a considerable amount of contempt and hostility from the ungodly, for such words as *brahmadvish*,[2] "hater of devotion," and *piyâru*,

did not follow Âryan rites, but were in the same condition as the Vrâtyas described by him in p. 33, and by Prof. Aufrecht at pp. 138 f. of the same volume, who were admissible by a particular rite within the Brahmanical pale. From Atharva Veda, v. 22, 14, however, it would appear that the Magadhas were regarded by the writer with enmity, and the people designated in the verse before us as Kîkaṭas, are described as hostile or indifferent to Âryan rites. (See Sanskrit Texts ii. 362 ff. and Wilson's note *in loco*.)

[1] As however it is said in the same verse that Indra subdues the terrible, and brings forward others, it is possible that these expressions may be meant merely to declare Indra's absolute control over the destinies of men, and to describe the Nemesis that overtakes pride, with an indication of the Herodotean idea τὸ θεῖον φθονερόν. (Herod. iii. 40; vii. 10, and 46.)

[2] This word *brahma-dvish* might mean either "hater of *priests*," or "hater of devotion," but in the R.V. it seems to have the latter sense. Sâyaṇa, on ii. 23, renders it *mantrâṇâm brâhmaṇânâm vâ dveshṭuḥ*, "hater of *mantras* (hymns), or of Brâhmans;" and similarly, on v. 42, 9, *brâhmaṇa-dveshṭrîn mantra-dveshṭrîn vâ*, "hater of Brâhmans or of mantras;" whilst on iii. 30, 17, he explains it by *brâhmaṇa-dvesha-kâriṇe*, "hater of Brâhmans;" and the same on vi. 22, 8; vi.

"despiser," which seem to be sometimes applied to irreligious Âryas, express something more than passive opposition. It may perhaps be further gathered from a few passages, which I shall now cite, that the recognized Âryan worship of the national gods, Agni, Indra, Varuṇa, etc., was not kept free from a certain admixture of demonolatry borrowed most probably from the aboriginal tribes; and it is indeed easy to conceive, or even a thing to be assumed as natural and necessary, that the religion as well as the language, manners, and customs of the Âryans should, in process of time, have undergone some modification from the close contact into which they must have been brought with these barbarous neighbours.[1]

From the first text which I shall quote, and which is ascribed by tradition to the rishi Vasishṭha, it seems that that distinguished personage himself had been accused, whether truly or falsely, of worshipping false gods, of familiarity with evil spirits, and the practice of devilish arts. A charge of this kind could scarcely have been made with any chance of being credited, unless such demonolatry was commonly known to have been practised either by him, or by other members of the same community. The passage referred to (R.V. vii. 104, 12 ff.) is as follows: "The intelligent man can easily discern, (when) true and false words contend together, which of them is true, and which of them is correct. Soma protects the former, and destroys untruth. 13. Soma does not prosper the sinner, nor the man who wields royal power deceitfully.

52, 3; vii. 104, 2; viii. 45, 23; and viii. 53, 1. The context of ii. 23, 4; v. 42, 9; vi. 52, 2, 3; x. 160, 4, seems to be in favour of the sense "haters of devotion," and the other passages contain nothing inconsistent with this interpretation. No use can therefore be made of this word to prove the importance of priests in the Vedic age.

[1] The demons mentioned in the Rig-veda are called by various names, such as *Rakshas*, *Yâtu*, *Yâtudhâna*, of which the feminine Yâtudhânî is also found, and apparently also *Dasyu* and *Dâsa*. The word *piśâchi* (masculine) also occurs in R.V. i. 133, 5, and *piśâcha* frequently in the A.V. The *Yâtus* are conceived as of different kinds, *śva-yâtu*, *ulûka-yâtu*, *susulûka-yâtu*, *koka-yâtu*, *suparṇa-yâtu*, *gṛdhra-yâtu*, the dog-, owl-, vulture-, etc. etc. formed Yâtus (vii. 104, 22); and *śapháruj yâtus*, perhaps, such as wound with their hoofs (x. 87, 12). Indra and Agni are the destroyers of the Yâtus who seek to disturb and vitiate the sacrifices and to slay these deities (vii. 104, 18, 20 f.; x. 87, 9 ff.). The Yâtus are described as devouring, insatiable, eaters of raw flesh, of the flesh of men and cattle, drinkers of milk, haters of devotion, maleficent, glaring-eyed, furious, the offspring of darkness (vii. 104 and x. 87 passim).

He slays the Rakshas, he slays the liar, they both sleep in the fetters of Indra. 14. If I am either one whose gods are false,[1] or if I have conceived of the gods untruly;—why art thou angry with us, o Jâtavedas; let slanderers fall into thy destruction. 15. May I die to-day if I am a Yâtudhâna, or if I have injured any man's life. Then let him be separated from his ten sons, who falsely addresses to me (the words) 'o Yâtudhâna.' 16. He who addresses to me who am no Yâtu[2] (the words), 'o Yâtudhâna,' or who (being) himself a Rakshas says, 'I am pure;'[3] let Indra slay him with his mighty bolt; let him sink down the lowest of all creatures." Sâyaṇa in his note on v. 12 refers to a legend according to which a Râkshasa had taken the form of Vasishṭha, and killed a hundred sons of that rishi, and that these verses were uttered by Vasishṭha to repel the charge of his having been possessed by the demon. This legend, however, which was no doubt manufactured to explain the verses, does not in reality answer this purpose. And it would seem, as I have above assumed, that Vasishṭha, or the speaker in these verses, whoever he may have been, had been charged with worshipping false gods, and with being under the influence of demons; and that while repelling the accusation, he here retorts upon his accuser by calling *him* a Rakshas.

Again in vii. 34, 8, the rishi says: "I who am no Yâtu (undemoniacal) invoke the gods; fulfilling (the ceremony) in due form, I offer a hymn." In another place[4] (vii. 21, 5) it is said: "Neither, o Indra, have Yâtus inspired[5]

[1] *Anṛta-devaḥ:* i.e. *asatya-bhûtâ devâ yasya,* "one whose gods are untrue, or unreal" (Sâyaṇa). Prof. Goldstücker *s.v.* interprets the word as meaning, "one to whom the gods are untrue." Prof. Max Müller renders the phrase, "If I had worshipped false gods." Prof. Roth who had originally *s.v.* taken the word to mean "a false prayer." withdraws this sense, and adheres to that given by Sâyaṇa, at the close of his article on *deva*.

[2] Roth *s.v.* explains the word *ayâtu* as meaning, "not demoniacal, free from demoniacal (magic)." Goldstücker *s.v.* defines the word, "a no-demon, a being different from, or the reverse of, a fiend."

[3] See Prof. Goldstücker's Dict. *s.v. ayâtu*.

[4] Quoted with its context in Sanskrit Texts, iv. 345.

[5] Or, "impelled," *jûjuvuḥ*. This is the sense given by Roth *s.v.* who explains the words thus: "Demons do not impel us:" *i.e.* "We are not in league with demons." Compare *deva-jûta,* "god-inspired," or "god-impelled," applied to

us . . . . . .[1] Let the lord (Indra) triumph over the hostile race; let no priapic (or long-tailed) demons,[2] approach our ceremony."

In vi. 62, 8, a person characterized as *rakshoyuj* is devoted to the vengeance of the gods. The commentator explains the term as either "the lord, or the instigator, of demons, or a priest possessed of, or by, demons" (Rakshases).

In vii. 85, 1, the word *arakshas* is used in a sense perhaps akin to that of *ayâtu*: "I consecrate (or polish, *puntshe*) for you twain an undemoniacal (*arakshasam*) hymn, offering a libation of soma to Indra and Varuṇa." The same word is also employed in viii. 90, 8, where the Aṣvins are thus addressed: "Since we offer to you an undemoniacal gift (*râtim arakshasam*)," etc. Compare ii. 10, 5; v. 87, 9.

If we should assign to the words *Rakshaso devavîtau* in R.V. v. 42, 10 (a passage quoted above), the sense of "the sacrifice offered to a Rakshas," the preceding conclusions would be still further confirmed.

If such demonolatry really existed to any extent among the Âryas, it is quite conceivable (I throw this out as a mere conjecture), that the intense hatred of the evil spirits whom, under the appellations of Yâtudhânas, Rakshases, Asuras, etc., Agni, Indra, and other deities, are so frequently represented in the R. V. (i. 133; iii. 15, 1;

Viṣvâmitra in iii. 53, 9; and, on the other hand, *dasyujûtaya* in vi. 24, 8, where it is said: "Indra does not bow to the strong nor the firm, nor to the bold man *impelled by a Dasyu* (or evil spirit)."

[1] The sense of the following words *na vandanâ vedyâbhiḥ* is obscure.

[2] *Ṣiṣnadevâḥ*. The same word occurs in x. 99, 3: "When, irresistible, he conquered by his force the treasures of the (city) with a hundred gates, slaying the priapic (or long-tailed) demons." (See Sanskrit Texts, iv. 346). If this word *ṣiṣnadeva* is correctly rendered as above, the demons in question may have some affinity with the Gandharvas, who are represented as objects of apprehension in A.V. iv. 37, in consequence of their propensity for women, whom, though themselves hairy like dogs or monkeys, they attempted to seduce by assuming an agreeable form (vv. 11, 12). The author of the hymn accordingly wishes that they may be emasculated (v. 7). [Professor Aufrecht thinks that *ṣiṣnadevâḥ*, being a *bahuvrîhi* compound, must mean "lascivious" (*ṣiṣnam devo yeshâm*).] These Gandharvas are also described (vv. 8, 9) as *havir-adân*, "eaters of oblations." In A.V. xviii. 2, 28, the Dasyus (who must here be demons) are spoken of as mingling with the Pitris under the appearance of friends, though they had no right to partake in the oblations; and Agni is besought to drive them away from the sacrifice. Compare the disputes regarding the admission of Rudra to a share in sacrifices, Sanskrit Texts, iv. 203, 241, 312 ff.

vii. 13, 1; vii. 15, 10; vii. 104; viii. 23, 13; viii. 43, 26; x. 87; x. 187, 3, etc.) as destroying or chasing away from the sacrifices which they disturbed and polluted (vii. 104, 18; x. 87, 9, 11), may not have been inspired by the dread which the superstitious worshippers entertained of those goblins, so much as by the fact that they were rival objects of adoration for whom their votaries claimed a share in the oblations, whilst the adherents of the gods described their patrons as triumphing by their superior power over the hostile intruders, and their magical arts (vii. 104, 20, 21, 24; x. 87, 19).[1]

Is it possible to look upon Rudra as having been originally a demon worshipped by the aborigines as the lord of evil spirits, and subsequently introduced into the Aryan worship? And that he was then, as well as originally, supplicated to abstain from inflicting those evils of which he was regarded as the author, and flattered by being addressed as the great healer of those sufferings which had their origin in his malevolence? (See the reference made to the late Rev. Dr. Stevenson's paper on the "Ante-Brahmanical Religion of the Hindus," and to Lassen's Ind. Antiq. in Sanskrit Texts, iv. 344). His malignant, homicidal, and cattle-destroying character (R.V. iv. 3, 6; i. 114, 10, Sanskrit Texts iv. 339), assimilates him to the Rakshasas and Yâtudhânas (though it is true that they are not, as he is, specifically described as the inflicters of disease and death); and he is described in the Ṣatarudriya (Vâj. S. xvi. 8, 20), as having attendants (*satvânaḥ*), while in A.V. xiii. 4, 27, all the Yâtus are said to obey his commands, and in *v.* 25 of the same hymn he is declared to be death, and immortality, vastness (*abhvam*), and a Rakshas (*sa eva mṛtyuḥ so 'mṛtaṃ so 'bhvaṃ sa rakshaḥ*); and in xi. 2, 30 f., reverence is offered to his wide-mouthed howling dogs, and to his shouting, long-haired, devouring armies. It is true that in the 11th verse of the same hymn he is asked to drive away dogs and shrieking female (demons) with dis-

[1] Perhaps, however, it is unnecessary to resort to this supposition in order to account for the dread and hatred of Rakshases which prevailed in the Vedic age. Such horror and hatred of demons appear to be natural to men in a certain stage of civilization. See Lecky's History of the Rise and Progress of Rationalism, i. 17 f.

hevelled hair; that in A.V. iv. 28, 5, Bhava (a deity akin to, or identical with, Rudra) and Ṣarva are solicited to destroy the Yâtudhâna who uses incantations (compare x. 1, 23) and makes men mad; that in Vaj. 16, 5, Rudra is besought to drive away Yâtudhanîs; that in A.V. xi. 2, 28, Bhava is asked to be gracious to the sacrificer who has faith in the existence of the gods, and in *v.* 23 is said to destroy the contemners of the deities who offer them no sacrifice;—all of these latter traits being common to him with the other Vedic gods. If, however, Rudra really represents a god or demon borrowed by the Âryas from the aborigines, it was to be expected that when adopted by the former he would be invested with the general characteristics which they assigned to their other deities, and that his connection with the evil spirits, of whom he was originally the chief, should as far as possible be kept out of sight and ultimately forgotten.

It is true that this theory leaves unexplained the connection of Rudra with the Maruts, in conformity with which he ought to be the god of tempests. (See the extract from Weber's Ind. Stud. in Sansk. Texts, iv. 334 ff.). But Rudra may be a composite character, and modified by the addition of heterogeneous elements in the course of ages.

There is no proof in the Rig-veda that the introduction of the worship of Rudra, even if it was more recent than that of the other Vedic gods, was met with any opposition. But we find there are hints that the adoration of the Rudras or Maruts was regarded as an innovation. These deities are described in many places (see my paper, "Contributions to a Knowledge of Vedic Theogony," etc., p. 110), as the sons of Rudra and Pṛṣni, and might, therefore, be supposed to have had some connection with Rudra. In one passage, too, (R.V. vii. 56, 17), a cattle-destroying and homicidal character (*gohâ nṛhâ vadho vaḥ*), akin to his, is ascribed to them. On the other hand, they are frequently represented as in close relation with Indra; and in fact it is almost inevitable that these deities of the tempest should be associated with the Thunderer, who could scarcely fulfil his function as dispenser of rain without their co-operation. But there are some hymns, viz., the 165th, the 170th, and the 171st, of the first Maṇḍala, in which Indra is introduced as regarding them with jealousy, and as resenting the worship which was paid to them. Thus in i. 160, 6 ff., he boasts that he is quite independent of their aid, while they reply that their assistance had been of importance to his success in battle. (Compare viii. 7, 31, and viii. 85, 7; iv. 18, 11). Again, in i. 170, Indra, who complains (*v.* 3) that the rishi Agastya was despising him and neglecting his worship, is besought (*v.* 2) to come to terms with the Maruts, and to associate with them at the sacrifice (*v.* 5); and in i. 171, 4, the rishi asks forgiveness from the Maruts, because, through dread of Indra, he had discontinued the sacrifice which he had begun in their honour. From all this it would seem as if the worshippers of Indra had entertained some objection to the adoration of the Maruts, and ascribed to the god the aversion to it which they themselves entertained. If there is any truth in the hypothesis that Rudra may have originally been a deity or demon who was introduced from the worship of the aborigines into that of their Aryan conquerors, the same may have been the case with the Rudras or Maruts, the sons of Rudra. Only, if this be the fact, these gods have been transformed in character in the course of their reception into the Indian pantheon, and rehabilitated by the ascription to them of different functions and milder attributes than those which belonged to them as deities, or demons of the aborigines.

The supposition which I have here made of the gradual transformation of Râkshasas into deities, is illustrated by the story told in the Mahâbhârata of the Râkshasî Jarâ, who is called a household goddess, and is represented as seeking to requite by benefits the worship which was paid to her. (See Sanskrit Texts, iv. 247).

I have already quoted from the Atharva-veda (v. 17) some evidence of the greater development which the Brahmanical pretensions had received subsequently to the age when the greater part of the Rig-veda was composed. Farther illustration of the same point may be found in the two hymns which follow the one just referred to, viz., A.V. v. 18, and

v. 19, which have been already translated in my former paper, "Miscellaneous Hymns from the Rig and Atharva Vedas," pp. 34 ff.). There is another section of the same Veda, xii. 5, in which curses similar to those in the last two hymns are fulminated against the oppressors of Brâhmans. The following are specimens: "4. Prayer (*bráhmán*) is the chief (thing); the Brâhman is the lord (*adhipati*). 5. From the Kshattriya who takes the priest's cow, and oppresses the Brâhman, (6) there depart piety (*sûnṛta*), valour, good fortune, (7) force, keenness, vigour, strength, speech, energy, prosperity, virtue, (8) prayer (*brahman*), royalty, kingdom, subjects, splendour, renown, lustre, wealth, (9) life, beauty, name, fame, inspiration and expiration, sight, hearing, (10) milk, juice, food, eating, righteousness, truth, oblation, sacrifice, offspring, and cattle;—(11) all these things depart from the Kshattriya who takes the priest's cow. 12. Terrible is the Brâhman's cow, filled with deadly poison. . . . 13. In her reside all dreadful things and all forms of death, (14) all cruel things, and all forms of homicide. 15. When taken, she binds in the fetters of death the oppressor of priests and despiser of the gods." A great deal more follows to the same effect, which it would be tiresome to quote.

I subjoin some further texts of the Atharva-veda in which reference is made to priests (*bráhmán*) and Brâhmans, and as I suppose these two words had by this period become nearly synonymous, there will no longer be any sufficient reason for separating the passages in which they respectively occur.

iv. 6, 1. "The Brâhman was born the first, with ten heads and ten faces. He first drank the soma; he made poison powerless." [1]

In xix. 22, 21 (= xix. 23, 30) it is similarly said: "Powers are assembled, of which prayer (or sacred science, *brahman*) is the chief. Prayer in the beginning stretched out the sky.

[1] I may mention for the benefit of any Indian Student who may see this article that this hitherto undiscovered variety of Brâhman, who was never anything but a "sky-flower," created by the prolific imagination of the author of this verse, was not again heard of, as far as I am aware, till he was resuscitated as Râvaṇa by the author of the Râmâyaṇa and his followers, who describe the enemy of Râma and ravisher of Sîtâ as a monstrous Brâhman with ten heads.

The *priest* (*brăhmăn*) was born the first of beings. Who, then, ought to vie with the *priest?*"

A superhuman power appears to be ascribed to the priest in the following passages,—unless by *priest* we are to understand Bṛhaspati :—

xix. 9, 12. "May a prosperous journey be granted to me by prayer, Prajâpati, Dhâtri, the worlds, the Vedas, the seven rishis, the fires; may Indra grant me felicity, may the *priest* (*brahman*) grant me felicity."

xix. 43, 8. "May the *priest* conduct me to the place whither the knowers of prayer (or of sacred science) go by initiation and austerity. May the *priest* impart to me sacred science."

The wonderful powers of the Brahmachârin, or student of sacred science, are described in a hymn (A.V. xi. 5), parts of which are translated in my paper on the progress of the Vedic Religion, pp. 374 ff.

And yet with all this sacredness of his character the priest must be devoted to destruction, if, in the interest of an enemy, he was seeking by his ceremonies to effect the ruin of the worshipper.

v. 8, 5, "May the *priest* whom these men have placed at their head (as a *purohita*) for our injury, fall under thy feet, o Indra; I hurl him away to death" (compare A.V. vii. 70, 1 ff.).